L

THE LEADERSHIP LIBRARY

VOLUME 6

WHAT EVERY PASTOR NEEDS TO KNOW ABOUT MUSIC, YOUTH, AND EDUCATION

THE LEADERSHIP LIBRARY

Volume

6

*What Every Pastor
Needs to Know about*

Music, Youth and Education

Garth Bolinder
Tom McKee
John R. Cionca

Carol Stream, Illinois

WORD BOOKS
PUBLISHER
WACO, TEXAS
A DIVISION OF
WORD, INCORPORATED

WHAT EVERY PASTOR NEEDS TO KNOW
ABOUT MUSIC, YOUTH, AND EDUCATION

© 1986 Christianity Today, Inc.

A LEADERSHIP/Word Book. Copublished by Christianity Today, Inc., and Word, Inc. Distributed by Word Books

Cover art by Joe Van Severen

Library of Congress Cataloging-in-Publication Data

Bolinder, Garth, 1948-
  What every pastor needs to know about music, youth,
and education.

  (The Leadership library ; v. 6)
  Includes bibliographical references.
  1. Pastoral theology—Addresses, essays, lectures.
2. Church music—Addresses, essays, lectures. 3. Church
work with youth—Addresses, essays, lectures.
4. Christian education—Addresses, essays, lectures.
I. McKee, Tom, 1941-   . II. Cionca, John R.,
1946-   . III. Title. IV. Series.
BV4013.B65 1986 253 86-1559
ISBN 0-917463-09-9
Bolinder, Garth, 1948-

Printed in the United States of America

CONTENTS

INTRODUCTION

Some elements of church ministry a pastor must handle personally—preaching, for instance, or performing weddings, funerals, and baptisms. For other elements, however, pastors often must oversee others who are "doing" the ministry. This is a book about the three areas where pastors are most likely managers rather than doers.

Whether done by full-time or part-time staff, or by volunteer workers, the tasks of music ministry, youth program, and Christian education demand the pastor's *in*direct involvement. Of course, pastors still find themselves on the line when there's a breakdown.

"When church ministry is going well, there's not that much interest in the machinery of how it happens," said one Nebraska pastor. But when choir members start feuding over where the robes will be stored, when parents complain the youth sponsors spend too much time discussing "Love, Sex, and Dating" and not enough in Scripture (or vice versa), or when two Sunday school teachers want to change the entire church's curriculum, suddenly pastors find themselves—and everyone else—studying the machinery.

They have to manage the church's specialty areas even

when they are not specialists. Why? Because specialty areas have a way of affecting the overall atmosphere. People leave churches more often not because of profound theological differences but because of worship styles, musical tastes, or dissatisfaction with the ministry to their children.

"What stifles worship in the church is not lack of creativity but fear of repercussions," said one minister. "The pastors I know aren't asking, 'What should our worship or music be?' but 'How long will we suffer if we change something?' We had to call an elders meeting to discuss changing the order of service!"

Most pastors are more comfortable ministering *to* others; this book asks, "How do you effectively minister *through* others?"

Some pastors admit to being autocrats, never relinquishing any real control. They tend to err on the side of retaining ultimate responsibility for virtually every decision. They allow staff or volunteers to handle routine details, and they'll show understanding and appreciation for initiative in peripheral areas as long as nothing threatens the position of pastor as *the* leader, the one who sets the direction for ministry.

Other pastors, however, take the opposite approach, delegating complete responsibility and authority for a particular ministry and assuming that's the end of their involvement. These pastors confess that their tendency is to leave staff members on their own to fly or to flop. Meetings are infrequent, supervision sparse, and planning sporadic. Decisions are made independently. What suffers is the unity of purpose, the philosophy of ministry, the coordinated strategy.

This book deals with the realities of local-church life and striking a balance between too much control and too little support. It shows how the gospel is to be at the center of all relationships, that even while ministering *through* others, pastors can have a ministry *to* them as well. In short, this volume is a simple, general overview of the dynamics of a ministry of overseeing.

Divided into three sections, it offers options for effectively getting the job done in ministries of music, youth, and Christian education.

Each section covers such topics as:

Why this ministry is crucial to church health.

The different ways of staffing this area.

The basic knowledge of the field a pastor needs to make sure the job gets done.

What roles the pastor can take in planning, directing, and controlling.

The keys to recruiting, motivating, equipping, training, and sustaining those responsible for the ministry.

How to maintain quality control.

What things are most likely to go wrong, and how to prevent or repair them.

Each section is written by a pastor who knows the specialty but has also experienced the practical problems of having to be a generalist and balance *all* the specialties of the church.

Garth Bolinder has had a lifelong interest in music—and married a musician—but is a pastor who has worked with full-time, part-time, and volunteer music ministers and musicians. He is currently senior pastor at Modesto (California) Covenant Church.

Tom McKee, for thirteen years a youth pastor, is now senior pastor of Sun River Church in Rancho Cordova, California. He sees ministry to teens *and their parents*, especially the growing numbers of single parents, as a key element of church life.

John R. Cionca brings to the area of education both academic (a Ph.D) and experiential credentials (eleven years as minister of Christian education). But he wrote these chapters while serving as senior pastor of Southwood Baptist Church in Woodbury, New Jersey.

Each of these men writes in nonspecialist language the essentials of the specialty—what every pastor needs to know about music, youth, and Christian education.

— Marshall Shelley
Senior Editor
Leadership

PART I
MUSIC

O N E
THE MAJESTY AND MISERY OF MUSIC MINISTRY

Garth Bolinder

The church board meeting was going long into the night. Fatigue and frustration were raising tempers to the boiling point. Finally, one rather rotund gentleman rose to his feet in red-faced exasperation.

"How long do we have to put up with this nonsense?" he demanded as his fist pounded the long oak table with a resounding thud. "We've tried and tried to be cooperative, but he just won't listen. Let's face it. He's impossible, and his music is even worse."

"Well, I think we ought to give him a chance," responded the thoughtful-looking gentleman in the corner. "At least he's concerned that worship be . . ."

"And what do you know about worship?" snorted the first man, his bulbous nose pulsating. "You're new here. You don't know how things are done."

"My wife says he's too demanding with the children. She says the kids don't even want to go to Junior Choir anymore," chirped a bespectacled man in a long coat.

"If he'd just play some of the old familiar hymns once in a while. Those new tunes are so difficult to sing. When he gets going on that instrument, it seems like he's in another world."

"Well, what do we do?" asked the chairman, trying to keep a semblance of order.

"My wife thinks he should have the decency to leave on his own accord, for the sake of the children."

"He oughta be fired," challenged the rotund one.

"We can't. He's under contract," the chairman interjected.

"Then let's send him a written ultimatum that tells him in no uncertain terms he's under probation. He either gets with our program or he's out. Don't you agree, Pastor?"

Now we don't know if the board meeting *actually* happened like that, but we do know a stern letter was sent through Dr. Deyling to the music minister. It was dated February 16, 1730. The recipient was a hard-working musician employed by a local church in Leipzig. His name? Johann Sebastian Bach.

Today it seems ludicrous to imagine J. S. Bach creating a stir with his contemporary Christian music. He's considered to be classical and "long hair." Many hail him as the greatest musician who ever lived.

Does not this ruckus illustrate the dilemma of the wedding of music and the church? Often they can't seem to live together, but certainly they can't live apart. Anyone in pastoral ministry has felt the tension of this holy alliance. We've soared to glorious heights at the Christmas cantata and sunk beneath the depths when the phone began ringing the next week. Somewhere between musicians and congregation, between heavenly aspiration and earthly reality stands the pastor. Whether in a small church with all volunteer musicians, or overseeing a miniconservatory in a megachurch, pastors are the catalysts for the music ministry. If music is going to thrive, it must begin with us.

You may be an accomplished musician, able to sight-read, vocalize, and arrange with the best. Or you may be at the other end of the scale, the only instrument you play being the radio. Your church may have an acclaimed music program, or it may leave much to be desired. As your choir sings every Sunday you may exclaim, "Now that's music!" Or you may mutter under your breath, "That's music?"

I don't claim to be a great musician. I write as a pastor. But I do love music. It lifts me, instructs me, soothes me, and even heals me in my journey Homeward. As I better understand its ministry, my appreciation grows. The church I serve doesn't claim musical superiority. But we are continually discovering its beauty, simplicity, and power.

What follows, then, is a plainsong on the joys and trials of music ministry. You're invited to join in. Seeking to improve our respective ministries is a worthy pursuit. For since the morning stars sang together, music ministry has been here to stay.

TWO

SETTING
THE TEMPO

Garth Bolinder

I t is easy for a pastor to be intimidated by the jargon and artistic flair of musicians. Nevertheless, every pastor must be aware that the key to music's effectiveness in the church is still in his hand. Music can have, indeed must have, a place in the larger ministry of the church. In a culture bombarded with musical sounds around the clock, it is crucial that pastors develop a clear perspective.

But this creates a dilemma for the overbusy minister. As Samuel A. Devan writes, the pastor ". . .is expected to combine the financial acumen of John D. Rockefeller, the spiritual fervor of St. Bernard of Clairvaux, the scholarship of Spenger, the organizing ability of a German bureaucrat, the aggressiveness of Napoleon, the smoothness of a politician, the tenderness of a parent, the magnetism of Lloyd George, the manners of Chesterfield, with the literary force of St. Paul, and the evangelistic impetus of John Wesley. It is hardly to be wondered at if occasionally some individual falls a little short of expectations in some of these particulars."[1]

And he didn't even mention music! What's a pastor to do? How can we find time and energy to add yet another area of expertise to our load? I've found the following three principles most helpful.

Take a Personal Inventory

The starting point is a personal evaluation of one's own perspective on music ministry.

Several years ago a young man came up to me and said, "When are we going to sing some 'Spirit-filled' songs on Sunday evening?"

When I asked him what he meant (I thought I already knew), he responded, "Well, I was thinking of some of the new praise choruses. They're the ones the Lord's using today."

Indeed! Give me a praise chorus anytime. Sing them over again to me. But don't forget to throw in some great hymns of the church. Then there's the Gloria Patri or the Kyrie eleison. An antiphon or two wouldn't hurt. And what about a Gregorian chant? Just what is the Lord using today, anyway?

Early in my ministry I probably would have enthusiastically agreed with my young friend. Since my own musical tastes were rather limited, it was only natural to use what "felt" good to me. Besides, those new choruses were upbeat, exciting, and they even sounded like some popular songs on the radio. Let's get relevant, anyway.

In seminary I learned precious little on church music. Though the trend seems to be changing now, few seminaries offered much in the field—especially evangelical schools, because of their proper concern for biblical truth. When I asked some pastoral colleagues how much they knew about the development of music in the church, they gave telling responses:

"I never thought about it before."

"I had enough trouble with church history. Besides, I can't sing very well."

"I let my music minister worry about that sort of thing."

"You mean they haven't always sung the Doxology after the offering?"

Those responses are probably typical for most of us. When it comes to music ministry, we don't know where we've come from and we may not know where we're going. We just know there has to be something better.

I began to realize the importance of pastoral leadership when I was asked about my philosophy of music ministry. My what? It was then pointed out to me that I was in a rut. That was the beginning of my personal evaluation. It led to a personal growth that is still continuing.

Personal evaluation begins with a series of questions. Though there is no system for grading answers, they help clarify our own personal perspective on music and its ministry in the church.

What styles of music do you most enjoy? When you listen to music at home, in the study or the car, what kinds are most common?

If you choose the hymns for worship, what is your criteria for selection?

If you do not choose the worship hymns, why not?

Do you keep a record of hymn usage in worship? What does the record indicate about your preference?

How many unfamiliar hymns has your congregation sung in the past year?

How well do you know the hymnal you use? Do you study its hymns, their meaning and use?

How often do you meet with your minister of music or choir director, accompanists and/or other musicians and soloists to plan, share your ideas, get theirs, and discuss the direction of the music ministry?

What is your personal church tradition? Are you from a liturgical background, emphasizing more ordered worship, classical music and restrained dignity? Or have you grown up with nonstructured worship, spontaneous songs and choruses (some composed right on the spot), and enthusiastic emotional release? Are you somewhere in the middle?

Think back to times when you have been deeply moved and ministered to by music. What caused this? Was it the music, the musician, the setting, or your own personal involvement and response?

What is your musical experience and/or training?

How important is music to your family, particularly your spouse? What are their tastes?

Honest answers to the above questions will help us get a handle on the opinions, circumstances, and pressures that shape our current perspective on music ministry.

During my first few years in the pastorate, I seemed to choose the ancient Irish hymn "Be Thou My Vision" almost every other month. It's a great hymn—but we were singing it into the ground. My wife finally pointed out what was happening, and I began to analyze why.

I remembered the first time I heard that beautiful song. I was in seminary and was going through some severe doubts about my call to ministry and my ability to be of any value if I was called. I struggled with this for several months. (Maybe taking Hebrew had something to do with my malaise; I don't know.)

One morning in seminary chapel, we closed with "Be Thou My Vision." As we sang that lilting Irish melody, I felt the clouds of depression break and a brilliant ray of hope break through. It was as if Jesus was ministering directly to me, using that hymn to heal me of my preoccupation with my own failure. In that very personal moment, my vision was restored and refocused on the goodness, sufficiency, and love of the Lord.

But that doesn't mean that I should have expected the same of my congregation, especially every other month!

Understanding the subtle yet powerful influence of our own limited personal perspective is a fundamental first step to getting our musical bearings. Next comes an evaluation of our congregation.

Don't Get Trapped

No two churches are alike. Regardless of proximity or denominational affiliation, they illustrate that God the Creator delights in diversity. Thus, there's no such thing as "Ninety-nine Sure-fire Methods to Guarantee a Successful Music Ministry or Your Money Back." Your congregation is unique, which can be either a blessing or a curse depending largely on your attitude.

Here are some pits I've fallen into and climbed back out of along the way:

1. *Unfairly comparing our music ministry with those of other churches.* I said *unfairly*, because we all compare to some degree. But woe to us if we fall into the trap of thinking our churches are inferior if we don't have the music that packs 'em in at the church across town.

2. *Running ahead of the congregation's ability to grow.* Let's be honest: Pastors are called to dream great dreams, to hear great themes. But if we run too fast and push too hard, we may find ourselves leading a lot of singing and singing a lot of solos (much to our chagrin and the church's).

3. *Settling for less than excellence.* I didn't say *less than perfection.* Perfectionism is a hobgoblin of creativity. But excellence should always be a personal and corporate value. Holy shoddiness is still shoddy. As the apostle Paul concluded his instructions on music ministry to the church at Colossae, he exhorted, "Whatever you do, whether in word or deed, do it all in the name of the Lord Jesus, giving thanks to God the Father through him" (3:17).

Several years ago I managed to fall into all three of these pits in one horrendous Sunday evening service. I had decided our music was dull. Even though we tried for variety, each week seemed to deepen my felt rut. Perhaps it was because we had a fair number of faithful elderly people at that service. Perhaps I was the problem. I really didn't know what the source was, but I was determined to do something about it.

After all, why couldn't we be like those really alive churches with their uninhibited exuberance and excitement? I'd heard they played and sang for hours, and nobody seemed to mind. In fact, people swarmed to their services, especially young people.

So we changed things that night. No more old hymns; only choruses. The guitars and bass seemed to help. But I knew something was wrong when I asked the congregation to link arms and sway as we sang. I could see on their faces they really weren't too thrilled about acting out their oneness in Christ. They'd be content just to sit and sing quietly about it, then go live it out (which they did) during the week.

My attempt to be upbeat and relevant turned out to be tacky and embarrassing. I had unfairly compared our music to "theirs." I had grossly outrun the ability of those fine people to change and grow. I had settled for enthusiasm over excellence. It was a rousing failure.

Still, I believe it's better to attempt something great and fail than to attempt nothing and succeed. For every musical success there are scores of missed notes, discarded manuscripts, and bungled refrains. As any musician (and pastor!) knows, practice and perseverance are great virtues.

Keep Looking for Buried Treasure

Some pits turn into gold mines. Every church has musical assets. Here are some ways to find them:

1. *Probe your minister of music or volunteer leader for his/her personal philosophy of music in the church.* Find out the history of music in this congregation. What's been done before? What are we trying to do today? The majority of churches have part-time music ministers, many of whom are faithful and have probably been at the church longer than the pastor. Regardless of their musical abilities, find out what makes them tick. You'll not only learn about them, you'll learn about the church as well.

2. *Take a look at your choir music library.* This will give you an idea of what the church is used to hearing. It will also reveal the taste of your minister of music and his or her predecessors.

3. *Do an inventory of instruments in the church* (unless, of course, your tradition does not use them). Find out their condition. What is available besides organ and piano?

4. *Make a list of all possible musicians in the church.* Who are the soloists? Who should be a soloist but isn't? Who is a soloist but

shouldn't be? Who plays what instruments? What are the special groups that sing or play? Don't assume that all the musicians have already surfaced.

One newer member of our church is a young mother who has a fine voice and communicates a beautiful radiance when she sings. Yet she told our minister of music she never sang in a previous church. Why? Probably because nobody took the time to develop a musical talent/gift list and then use it.

5. *Pay special attention to accompanists.* These dedicated people are usually hidden behind a keyboard. They help the soloists; they support the congregation; but rarely do they get much attention until they hit a wrong note. Get to know them, encourage them, and find more people to help them. Don't be afraid to pay them. When music purchases and practice times are figured in, most accompanists are excellent bargains.

6. *Look at your music budget and see if it is realistic.* Music material costs are up. Seminars and workshops aren't free. Choir robes need to be cleaned and/or replaced. There's no such thing as discount music ministry.

7. *Study the musical climate of your community.* Evaluating this can help you better understand congregational opinions and expectations.

8. *Begin where you are and grow from there!* Both covetous yearning and self-satisfied complacency lead in the same direction: inertia. If the music ministry of your church is going to grow, the pastor must be committed to helping it happen.

One of the steps I've taken to expand my comprehension is to do a topical word study on music in the Bible. The usage and meaning of such terms as *music, singing, singers, songs, instruments, psalms,* and *choirs* stretched my awareness of the centrality of music in the story of God's people.

Among the books on music ministry, I recommend *Jubilate! Church Music in the Evangelical Tradition* by Donald P. Hustad.[2] This well-written book provides historical survey, biblical foundations, contemporary music ministry suggestions, and resources for further study.

I've also been challenged simply by listening to other

people talk about music—their feelings, likes and dislikes, dreams and desires. I've dug into hymnology using the companion volumes some publishers provide that give short histories of hymns, their composers, and ways to utilize hymns for the good of the church. Naturally, the more I utilize the topical headings of our church's hymnal, the more my choices are purposeful and informed.

You don't have a minister of music? Don't give up—there's hope. Somewhere is a person who can lead your church in this area. Some churches go outside the membership to recruit a music leader. This means providing a salary, even if the work requires only a few hours per week. Such a person usually has some musical background and/or training and can direct the choir, assist in worship leading, maybe even play an instrument. If this person works closely with the pastor, music ministry can thrive.

But many churches may not be able to afford a hired music minister. What then?

Start looking within the congregation. A treasure may be waiting to be discovered. Our experience is an encouraging example of God's delightful provision. A little more than ten years ago, Modesto Covenant Church had a struggling choir of about twelve and no one to lead them. Music ministry was a faint diminuendo.

Furthermore, the church was between pastors. However, the retired interim pastor, Rev. C. D. Anderson, saw the need and decided to do something about it. He began to pray for a music minister. He asked several others to pray with him. After a time he decided to ask a rather new member, Lois Larson, if she would be interested.

Though she was a fine soloist with vocal training, she refused, pleading no experience in choral work.

The interim pastor went back to prayer. The more he prayed, the more convinced he became that Lois was the person for the job. He asked again and again. Now both Lois and her husband were praying. Was this a call from the Lord?

Eventually, she accepted the position on a temporary basis. As Lois tells the story, she was so nervous at the first rehearsal she had to stop in the middle because she was sure she was going to faint.

What happened to this tentative, nervous, temporary music minister? Today she directs a music ministry bursting at the seams. The adult choir has seventy committed singers. Excellent soloists, duets, trios, and quartets of every voice lead in worship Sunday after Sunday. Accompanists abound. Lois coordinates a musicale series each year that brings outstanding artists to the church, magnifying our outreach into the community. Perhaps most significant are the children's and youth choirs Lois oversees. Almost two hundred people from first grade through young adult meet weekly to sing, learn, and worship.

This wonderful story needn't be unique. The splendid music ministry we enjoy can be duplicated in churches everywhere, regardless of size. A supportive congregation led by a praying pastor committed to music ministry can find and nurture a music minister who will bless both congregation and community.

Martin Luther once said, "We must, of necessity, maintain music in schools. Neither should we ordain young fellows to the office of preaching except they have been well-exercised and practiced in the field of music."

Luther realized the mighty power of music in the ministry of the gospel. He knew that pastors hold the key to effective music in the churches. His attitude of appreciating and encouraging music may have had as much impact on the Reformation as did his theology. It was certainly evident in the life of a certain music minister in Leipzig.

Music historians tell us that curious letters can be found on many Bach manuscripts: "J.J." for *Jesu juva* ("Jesus, help me") at the beginning, and "S.D.G." for *Soli Deo gloria* ("To God alone be the glory") at the end. In between lies all music ministry.

Throughout his life Bach had to contend with pastors, most of them antagonistic. Imagine what would have happened if they had been supportive.

With Jesus as our Helper, our music ministry can continue to grow so God alone will get the glory.

---

1. Austin Lovelace and William Rice, *Music and Worship in the Church* (Nashville: Abingdon, 1976) p. 30.
2. Carol Stream, Ill.: Hope, 1981.

THREE

ADAGIO FOR A PASTOR: TOWARD CLOSER STAFF HARMONY

Garth Bolinder

I saw him coming. Like a runaway locomotive with steam billowing in all directions, he broke through the line of departing parishioners and screeched to a halt in front of me.

"What's the idea of changing the closing hymn this morning without telling me?" he demanded in a fortissimo voice. "I work so hard to plan the music and coordinate the service, then you have the nerve to throw that clinker in at the last minute."

"Clinker?" I responded weakly, trying to appear calm before the startled people around me. I was a young pastor; he was a talented musician. He was several years older than I, but we had never directly clashed before.

"That last hymn was a clinker! A terrible selection. The congregation couldn't sing it. The organist couldn't play it. And I didn't like it. It didn't fit at all. Never, never, do that again."

He turned abruptly and strode off, leaving me stunned as I mumbled something about the stress of ministry to the curious bystanders still in the hallway. Fumbling my way to the refuge of my office, the blessing of the morning quickly faded.

What began as bewilderment at the surprise attack turned rapidly to seething defensiveness.

Who does he think he is anyway? I thought angrily. *I have a right to do what's best for the worship service. After all, who's in charge here? I don't care if he has been at the church longer. Besides, that wasn't such a bad hymn. We used to sing it in seminary chapel all the time. He should talk. The choir's been eating into my preaching time the past seven Sundays, yet he still says we need two anthems. No wonder we get out late. Makes you wonder if a music ministry is worth it.*

Sound familiar? Whether you sympathize with my self-righteous indignation or my musical colleague's vocal frustration, you probably recognize the confrontation as fairly typical in the continuing duet between pastors and musicians. Though there are moments of sublime harmony, there are also times of painful dissonance as opinions, traditions, and egos clash.

Music has always been at the center of the worshiping community. It is one of God's most glorious gifts, able to move people beyond the realm of mere words. Without doubt, music touches the eternal. But many times we find it the center of temporal turmoil, even among God's people.

King David, that sweet singer of Israel, touched off controversy as he sang and danced the Ark of the Covenant into Jerusalem. We've all been tormented by self-appointed experts who regularly criticize the weekly choice of music. What pastor hasn't felt anxiety rising as the offertory soloist labors through six verses while sermon time is being diminished note by note?

Who is to decide the proper role of music in the church? Most ministers of music will say the responsibility is theirs. Most pastors will remind you that they still lead the church. Ask the congregation, and you'll get more opinions than Bach has cantatas.

Too often these conflicting attitudes and expectations can threaten the life of a local congregation. One pastor commented, "More churches have been split over worship styles, musical tastes, and service format than any other cause."

Is he right? Must music be a continual battleground between musicians and pastors? I think not. There is a better way, but it's not a quick formula to guarantee a spectacular music ministry.

Some congregations see music as a distant cousin to the "real" ministry of the church. And since they don't want to take responsibility for integrating it into the essential ministry of the church, they say, "Let's hire someone to do it for us." They sign up a music minister to dress up the services. As a result, services—and often the ministry itself—become more performance than participation. The people tend to become critics rather than worshipers. The music director becomes a producer rather than a minister, and the gap between minister and congregation only widens.

The pastor is forced to side with the congregation or the minister of music. If he chooses the congregation, a staff member is alienated. If he sides with the music director, his own ministry becomes more vulnerable to criticism.

Neither approach is the solution.

I prefer the adagio, that slow, steady movement that brings a strong, balanced calm to a symphony—or a church. Pastors can bring this calm, balanced strength through hard work, patience, and the skill of a conductor. I've found the following principles are part of such a composition.

Minister to, Not Just through Musicians

The musicians I know are real people with real needs, just like the rest of the parishioners (and just like the pastor!).

I've had the privilege of working with three different ministers of music. They've differed in their ages, gender, training, and abilities. They've been part-time and full-time. At times their musical tastes have been very different from mine, but they've all shared one common trait: commitment.

Sensitive, sometimes fickle, maybe even demanding, most music ministers I know see their ministry as a distinct calling. Yet they often struggle with the same things that hinder pastors—insecurity, feelings of inadequacy, and exhaustion. They need someone they can trust. They need a pastor.

Years ago I had the privilege of working with Norman Johnson, past editor at Singspiration and minister of music at the Evangelical Covenant Church in Grand Rapids, Michigan. Norm had been at the church for many years; I was a rather green seminary graduate. To me, Norm was almost legendary. His reputation and presence kept me in a certain state of awe those early years. His ministry left an indelible mark on my life and ministry.

Yet, more than once I was sure the church wasn't big enough for both of us. Fortunately, I learned an important lesson: Deep down, fame, ability, and commanding presence didn't mean that much to Norm. Friendship did.

I'll never forget several lunches we had at Norm's request. At the time he had recently been diagnosed as having A.L.S., a dreaded disease, and he needed companions. Suddenly my order of worship and choice of hymns seemed no longer important. Norm's heart was breaking. He needed a friend, someone who could listen. As Dietrich Bonhoeffer wrote, "Christians have forgotten that the ministry of listening has been committed to them by the One who is Himself the great listener and whose work they should share. We should listen with the ears of God that we may speak the Word of God."

I'm not sure if there was a song leader in that happy, calamitous band that traveled with Jesus, but if there was, I'm sure he knew he could share his burdens with his Master, whom he knew would listen.

I also suspect Jesus was more than willing to share a laugh with his disciples. More and more I'm convinced that ministry to colleagues means sharing glad times as well as struggles. Laughing together is a life-giving exercise.

Malcolm Muggeridge once commented that the steeple and the gargoyle of the medieval cathedral provide a healthy pattern for the Christian life, the steeple symbolizing the heart reaching for the infinite God in heaven while the laughing gargoyle reminds us of our earthbound limits. What a pattern for healthy co-ministry relationships! We needn't take ourselves overseriously. Amid the urgency of our task, the joy of shared laughter can lighten heavy loads, calm ruffled feelings, refresh weary pilgrims, and renew an eternal perspective.

In our church, our staff will lunch together for any special occasion we can find. Practical jokes are a part of our normal week. Seasonal staff get-togethers are regular. Good relationships must be worked at, but the result is worth the effort. Mutual concern and joy are contagious. Our congregation is encouraged to see that its staff not only *works* well together but actually enjoys *being* together.

Listening and laughter are two gifts any pastor can offer. Musicians, like anyone else, care about ministry because they've received a ministry of care. Belonging is the foundation of all motivation.

Fix the End; Flex the Means

People tend to work better, certainly more enthusiastically, when you clearly establish the end but allow freedom to develop the means. As Peters and Waterman said in *In Search of Excellence*, people are motivated by a simultaneous need for both meaning and independence. Many times I've determined the meaning without allowing the corresponding independence to reach the end. Here again I learned a great lesson from Norman Johnson.

Like most seminary graduates, I approached my first parish keenly aware of the inadequacies of the church and the solutions for solving them. It was a rather arrogant ignorance with a spiritual veneer. So I would plan great moments for the congregation where our worship could finally be what God intended for us to experience. I took particular care to select hymns of substance, structure, and style. No gospel fluff for us. Unfortunately, I wasn't aware of my rather limited knowledge of hymnody, nor of my ignorance of the tastes and abilities of the congregation. My wife, a music major in college, tried to alert me to such liabilities, but I thought pastor knew best.

Finally, Norm graciously reminded me that familiarity and

singability weren't sins. He worked with me to broaden my use of the hymnal, to be willing to incorporate hymns that may be less sophisticated, yet still to strive for excellence in worship. Gently I was reminded that he knew the territory better than I.

Not only have I found music ministers more knowledgeable than I, they are often more creative. I've learned to heed their creative ideas.

Several years ago during Advent, our minister of music, Lois Larson, decided to have the Christmas choir concert in our fellowship hall. She wanted people to invite unchurched friends who might not come to a church service but would come to a more intimate evening of music, hot cider, and cookies. Our fellowship hall, however, when tightly seated, has about one-third the capacity of our sanctuary. This would mean at least three performances with tickets to regulate the crowds. Inwardly I shuddered, "Welcome to the Covenant Cabaret!" All I could think about were the logistical and ecclesiastical headaches.

O me of little faith. It was a splendid evening! Our unchurched friends seemed to enjoy it most. Again the lesson came home: Allow freedom for individual gifts to be expressed and grow. But do it within the context of structure. Planning is the key.

The more we strategize, the better we harmonize. Thus, regular staff meetings are a must. Regular calendar review, both long- and short-range, anticipates seasons and special events before they spring up as surprises.

Is it possible to give the music minister my preaching schedule for the next six (how about three) months? It is, and I'm amazed how much this helps. The choir doesn't have the pastoral luxury of waiting for last-minute inspiration to decide what to do on Sunday. They need weeks of rehearsal time. Musicians must plan ahead even if the pastor does not. Why not work together?

Such planning not only gives direction to the music ministry but also enhances corporate worship and probably makes for better preaching. It even eases the pastor's Saturday night nerves.

Encourage Musicians to Grow

Professional development and spiritual growth are crucial to any ministry, including music. Unless the pastor personally encourages such growth, it might not happen. Such encouragement is both direct and indirect.

First, the direct. A former colleague, a minister of music/Christian education, was an outstanding organist. On any given Sunday, I would find myself, in Charles Wesley's words, "lost in wonder, love, and praise" because of the glorious organ music that guided our worship. Regularly I thanked Glen for the hours he spent preparing and told him how much his ministry meant to me and to the congregation. He was successful in this area, and he needed to know it.

It's easy to focus on areas of weakness, thinking that correcting faults will lead to better performance, but success is usually a more powerful motivator than failure. After affirming strengths, then we can strengthen weaknesses based on a firm foundation of accomplishment. Direct, honest encouragement pays rich dividends.

Encouragement can also be indirect. I've found I need to be an ally, sometimes even an advocate, for music ministry to the church board. I'll push for increasing the budget so new music can be purchased regularly. I realize some feel the choir could still sing the old songs, but these same folks never want to hear the same sermon twice.

Freshness is part of encouraging creativity, and so I encourage musicians to improve their craft by attending seminars, workshops, and classes at the church's expense. Why not provide money for subscriptions to professional journals and music libraries?

Then, if the musicians are paid, there's the issue of salary. Here's where the baton hits the podium. Are we willing to recommend quality raises at annual review time? We know what raises do for us. The song is the same for ministers of music.

One last form of encouragement: Pray with and for the musicians. Often we relate on a solely professional level. They need prayer as much as anyone. Don't believe those who say there's no business like show business. Ministering week by week to a media-blitzed congregation is tough. Tastes run from Amy Grant to Giovanni Gabrielli. Musicians feel the pressure and need to know they're being prayerfully supported.

Dignify the Ministry of Music

To dignify the ministry of music, we must be willing to go public, to let the congregation know how valuable it is, to develop appreciation for the musicians. Corporate worship is prime time to affirm the work of musicians and ministers of music.

In our church, we offer a prayer of consecration at the beginning of each choir season. Regularly I refer to the anthems and solos (even to unsung accompanists) during worship. It's one thing to say "Nice anthem last Sunday" as we pass each other in the hall. It's something else to express it on Sunday morning from the pulpit.

Dare I mention applause? Always cautious to avoid the entertainment complex (after all, when will they ever clap after a sermon?), heartfelt applause out of adoration for God and appreciation for his gift of music can be a genuine form of public affirmation.

After being in my present church for about a year, I realized our minister of music had been faithfully serving for about eleven years. Technically only part-time, Lois had developed a splendid ministry, one that had a reputation perhaps larger than the church.

When I asked if the church had recognized her ten years of service, I received an embarrassed no. We went to work. A secret letter was sent to the congregation informing them of our surprise evening of recognition. That night, tributes were given. Then the lights went out. Suddenly Lois was flooded in a stream of light from the new spotlight the church purchased—something she had been wanting for five years. No more borrowing or renting.

The results were great. The congregation enjoyed showing public gratitude. Lois was thrilled, and the music ministry has become even better. Such is the value of giving the ministry of music the dignity it rightly deserves.

Even with all this, however, problems can still arise. I've found a need for at least one more principle.

Know When to Intervene

There are times in any organization when a part can run ahead or away from the rest. This can be true of music ministry in the church, usually the result of exuberance and enthusiasm. Rivers can overflow their banks; sometimes the pastor has to sandbag.

Knowing when to intervene is an art. It demands patience, wisdom, firmness, and love. Because people and situations are different, legal lists of what to do aren't too helpful. Instead, I've found it helpful to try seeing the situation two ways: through objective and subjective relationships.

Objectively, I'm concerned with the relationship of music ministry to the larger ministry of the church. Subjectively, I'm concerned with my relationship to the minister of music. Both must be weighed to solve any problem successfully.

Several years ago our high school choir performed a Christmas musical. The music was good, and the choreography was illustrative and lively, except for one piece about Herod's court. As I watched them practice, I kept waiting for John Travolta to strut down the aisle. It wasn't tasteless or obscene, but I could envision trying to explain our rendition of Sunday Night Fever.

Of course, the choir loved it, so if I were to intervene, I would risk offending and alienating them.

Private intervention always being best, I decided to talk

with Lois the next day. I said I wondered if some people might misunderstand the one number with its animated anatomical antics. She said she'd had the same concern. Because we both wanted what was best for the larger ministry of the church, we agreed on something that could have been a major conflict if either of us had had a narrower perspective. In this case, my intervention was timely and helpful.

Other times, however, intervention is a mistake. Early in my pastorate here in California, I decided to bring a different emphasis to Christmas. Instead of the annual Christmas Eve service the church was used to, I proposed a traditional Scandinavian *Julotta* service at 6 A.M. on Christmas Day.

My concerns were genuine but not well informed. Our minister of music was less than enthusiastic and pointed out that the Christmas Eve service was an opportunity for outreach; a 6 A.M. service probably was not. But I was adamant, so we went ahead and did it my way.

Frankly, the service was reasonably well attended, but it was dull and lifeless. I felt I was dragging everyone with me. I learned again that worship is corporate, not just individual. The pastor's taste and prerogative is not enough of a foundation on which to build.

Admitting that I misread the congregation and its needs has strengthened both my relationships and leadership within the church. Wise intervention by the pastor is occasionally needed in the continuing duet with the minister of music. The ability to admit unwise interventions is also a necessity.

Late one evening a number of years ago, I happened to walk into Norm Johnson's office as he was working on a new choir arrangement. I watched his intensity. Discarded first, second, third, and fourth drafts of the score he was trying to compose were scattered across the room.

"So this is how they make music, huh?" I commented, interrupting his concentration.

"The music," he said, "comes from the Chief Musician. I'm just trying to find it, and hard work is the only way I know."

Hard work indeed! So is the sustaining of music in the life of the church. The continuing improvisation between pastors and musicians will keep on going. Simplistic solutions are not to be found. But it's better to strive for a duet, not a duel in our service for the kingdom.

MUSIC IN WORSHIP

Garth Bolinder

My wife and I were seated high in the Minneapolis Civic Auditorium, where approximately seven thousand were celebrating our denomination's centennial. Up front, four choirs were leading in worship. To demonstrate both diversity and unity in Christ, the choirs were from Hispanic, Korean, anglo, and black churches.

At one point the black choir from Oakdale Covenant Church in Chicago burst into a rousing anthem that asked everyone to "stand up and be a witness for Jesus." Almost in unison, the entire centennial congregation stood, clapping and singing, to declare its solidarity as witnesses called of God.

Then the four choirs began to mingle in what seemed a chaos. To the pulpit came a pastor, who read the majestic words of Revelation 7, "After this I looked, and behold, a great multitude which no man could number, from every nation, from all tribes and peoples and tongues, standing before the throne and before the Lamb, clothed in white robes, with palm branches in their hands, and crying out with a loud voice, 'Salvation belongs to our God who sits upon the throne, and to the Lamb!' "

Suddenly the combined multi-ethnic choir exploded in the mighty words of Handel's "Hallelujah Chorus." Again the audience was on its feet. Some heads were bowed. Others were held high with hands outstretched. Radiant smiles were on faces and tears were in eyes. Hands were clasped as the entire company of believers joined in joyful, loving praise to the King of Kings and Lord of Lords. It was an eternal moment that illustrated music's incredible power, as Bach put it, to "glorify God and recreate the spirit."

Purpose

When we reflect on the life of God's people, both in Scripture and in church history, it is obvious that God loves music! From Jubal and his pipe and lyre in Genesis, through the musical hosts at the temple worship, through New Testament songs, hymns, and spiritual songs, to the heavenly choirs in Revelation, music has been at the center.

Though music has taken many forms and had many uses, worship has been its primary purpose. As Winfred Douglas said at the 1935 Hale Lectures at Seabury-Western Theological Seminary, "Worship is the primary and eternal activity of redeemed mankind."

William Temple wrote, "To worship is to quicken the conscience by the holiness of God, to feed the mind with the truth of God, to purge the imagination by the beauty of God, to open the heart to the love of God, to devote the will to the purpose of God."

According to Jesus, there is only one true object of worship: "You shall worship the Lord your God and him only shall you serve" (Matt. 4:10). Music is first and foremost a ministry of worship to God. It is a gift we bring to our heavenly Father. This radically affects the way we choose church music.

Several years ago, when living in New England, my children and I attended a concert by the Northeast Connecticut Concert Choir. My wife sang in that choir, as did several friends from our church. We sat next to a neighbor, a good friend, yet one who expressed little interest in Christianity.

The concert concluded with John Rutter's magnificent "Gloria." As the choir and orchestra blended voices and instruments in the words "Gloria, in excelsis Deo," a transformation took place. No longer was this just a proper Sunday afternoon concert for the culturally interested (and those who would leave television football early). The music swept us heavenward. The audience was awestruck.

The explosive applause at the end was more spontaneous agreement than appreciation. My neighbor friend turned to me with tears in his eyes. I, the pastor, and he, the agnostic, embraced in wordless affirmation. Music had been the bridge from the senses to the soul.

God alone is worthy to be praised. We are *made* to worship. If we really believe this, music will be a prepared offering, not a spiritual pacifier. As Austin Lovelace and William Rice write in *Music and Worship in the Church*, "Our gifts to the God who created us, sent his Son to us, and guides us by his Holy Spirit should be worthy of acceptance. If this be true, our gifts should represent some cost to us. A shallow hymn, a sloppily sung anthem, are hardly fit gifts to bring as an offering to God, for they cost us little or nothing. If more work is required to sing a better hymn or to prepare a finer anthem, should we do less than our best to bring a 'living sacrifice, holy and acceptable unto God, which is your spiritual worship?' "[1]

This attitude differs from our culture, which primarily sees music as a means of stimulating and/or soothing human emotion. It is largely feeling-oriented—which is too often our view of music in the church. The comments of several pastors I interviewed reflected this. A friend in Massachusetts felt music should prepare people for the message from the Word of God. Another pastor in Illinois commented that music should be contemporary in order to appeal to all types of people. Another spoke of the need to keep music plain so no one would be offended. A friend in California thinks music should "be exciting so people get excited about God."

All these may be important, but they pale in significance if our primary purpose is to give glory to God. Music ministry is more than "emotion, commotion, and promotion." From a trained, even paid, soloist singing a recitative from the *Messiah*, to a high school choir singing the latest contemporary Christian hit, to a young child singing "Jesus Loves Me" in the Sunday school Christmas program, the first priority of music ministry is singing unto the Lord. Any pastor, regardless of musical interest or ability, can encourage such a perspective in the church.

Lovelace and Rice offer the following criteria for worship music:

1. Does the music speak the feelings and thoughts of the true worshiper? Is it related to life itself?

2. Does the music express universal truths as well as individual emotions? Does the music help each individual to grow in Christian stature?

3. Does the music speak of eternal mysteries? Does the greatness of the music suggest the greater majesty of God?

4. Is the music creative in design and performance? Does it help make the time of worship one of new insights, new visions, and new approaches to God?

5. Have composer and performers assumed moral responsibility for creative integrity and excellence of craftsmanship in presenting the Word of God? [2]

I've found these questions important to ask, because they focus on why I do what I do. If I really believe, in Kierkegaard's well-used words, that God is the audience in worship, then everything I do and direct should be pleasing and honoring to him. One doesn't need to be a five-star chef to make sure the toast doesn't burn. I don't have to be an accomplished musician to make sure our musical offerings have integrity.

This positive attitude becomes contagious. I regularly get phone calls from soloists, youth choir directors, and even accompanists, asking if their choice of music (not only for Sunday mornings but Sunday evenings as well) is appropriate to the sermon theme or focus of the service. I've never insisted on such control. Rather, I think our folks are seeing the value of a clearly defined purpose in worship. They want to participate in harmony.

Planning

Of course, the more we plan, the more we want to plan. It takes work, but it's well worth the effort.

Planning is hard work. People will always resist it, including pastors. Once Martin Luther's friend and nemesis Andreas Carlstadt complained that it was unnecessary to spend time in music planning and hymn composition. He even objected to harmony, because there was only one faith, one Lord, one baptism.

To which Luther quipped, "Then Carlstadt should have only one eye, one ear, one foot, one knife, one coat, and one penny."

We need only to read about the great festivals of the Old Testament to realize the significant preparation necessary for divine worship.

There are many ways to plan. We each have our own system of aiming at the future. I've found I need to have regular meetings with all those associated with our worship services. Not only do we have weekly general staff meetings where we evaluate, brainstorm, and plan, but each week I meet with the minister of music to compare calendars, share ideas, review services, and focus on the future. We try to keep thinking six months ahead. And, yes, I need to be held accountable for this.

Of the several structures one can use, the most common ones seem to be the Christian year, the preaching schedule, and special events. Some churches use a combination. I mention the Christian year because it has the longest history. Formalized since the fourth century, it provides a New Testament parallel to the Old Testament cycles of feasts and remembrances. Thus the entire year is divided into the great redemptive themes of Advent, Christmas, Epiphany (what a splendid word!), Lent, Easter, and Pentecost.

Some evangelical churches may find this "too liturgical." Every tradition has its own liturgy, however. Even regular "sharing time" on Sunday nights is liturgical. So the question becomes "Why do we order our music and worship the way we do?"

Personally, I have a growing appreciation for the Christian year because it does, in Henri Nouwen's words, "shape our personal stories into the One True Story. Usually, we try to shape His Story into ours." So, even as I write these words, I'm reminded that the season is Pentecost, and I need the indwelling Spirit for guidance, creativity, and strength.

If you choose this method for worship planning, including music, the process becomes both ordered and exciting. Hymn selection, anthems, and special music are all influenced by the reason for the season. Within these guidelines, creativity emerges. Several years ago, during Advent, we used Sunday nights to walk through the Christian year. It was a novel experience for most of the congregation.

First we talked about the theme of redemption in the Old Testament and walked through the cycle of feasts and sacrifices, each one signifying a mighty divine intervention. We talked about the meaning of these events for the people of God. We even imagined their songs. Then we turned to the back of our hymnals and found the lectionary of seasons and Scriptures. We talked about the coming of the Messiah, the already and the not-yet. We sang Advent hymns about preparation and expectation. We read Scriptures of judgment and consolation, both Advent themes. We personalized the season, asking where we each needed to prepare the way for Messiah. Then we prayed, asking for a fresh divine visitation in our personal lives, our families, our jobs, our church, our community, our world.

It was marvelous! The services were simple. The hymnal

was our primary aid. No gimmicks were needed, because the story spoke for itself. Everyone from youngest child to oldest adult became both storyteller and story receiver during that season.

Canon Michael Green says a distinctive characteristic of the early church was its incessant "babbling" of the gospel. The people couldn't stop talking about Jesus. Ordering music and worship into the Christian year helps such holy and joyful babbling continue.

Another method of music planning revolves around preaching. As mentioned in the previous chapter, having a preaching schedule not only gives structure and security to the music minister but also helps the pastor plan and preach better. A preaching schedule insures that the preacher and musician are heading in the same direction. It guards against such ludicrous embarrassments as a sermon on temperance preceded by that lovely anthem "Ho! Everyone That Thirsteth."

Every week our music minister and I spend about a half hour evaluating and planning, each with sermon schedule in hand. What a harmonizer this is. She has a starting place from which to select appropriate music, and I get a preview of "coming attractions." Several weeks ago I found out Lois had chosen Tom Fettke's beautiful anthem "The Majesty and Glory of Your Name" to coordinate with my sermon on Creation. Knowing that this anthem would complement my message gave me renewed inspiration and encouragement. With the music running through my mind, sermon preparation became worship. I could hardly wait for Sunday to come so I could hear both anthem and sermon (even if I was preaching).

Special events, holidays, and recognition days also provide structures for music planning. Like many pastors, Ray McGinnis, a Free Methodist minister in western New York, has a special independence theme every year on the Sunday closest to July 4. Patriotic music and symbols are tastefully integrated into the larger biblical theme of freedom in Christ. Every time I've worshiped in such a service, especially in a rural church, I've come away grateful for the privilege/ responsibility of being a Christian in America in a needy world.

Planning gives purpose. Hymn selection becomes a meaningful exercise. Until several years ago, I relied on either my limited hymn knowledge or the suggestions of my music minister. Now I'm growing in my understanding and appreciation of hymnology. To do so is to realize that, while all hymns have some use, some have more use than others. Evangelicals seem to slide particularly toward hymns of sentiment rather than substance. We like hymns and choruses that speak about God or about our experience with him. Though the past decade has seen a renewal in praise choruses directed to God, I think there's great room for improvement in hymn use.

There's probably even room for more pastors to venture into the uncertain arena of hymn making. On several occasions I've written additional verses to hymns in order to tighten the connection with the theme of the sermon. I put such a verse in the bulletin, with no by-line. Hearing the entire congregation sing those new words gives me all the affirmation I'll ever need. (Who knows, maybe they think I've uncovered a rare manuscript?)

Resources abound to help the pastor interested in hymnology. Anything by Eric Routley is most helpful. His *Hymns and the Faith* (Seabury Press, 1956) is an excellent introduction into wise selection and use. Also very useful are two books by James Sydnor, *Hymns: A Congregational Study* and *Hymns and Their Uses*, both published by Hope.

I've been fascinated to sit down with our hymnal and study its rich contents. The categories, Scripture references, even composers and dates add insight into hymn origin and use. For instance, it's encouraging to remind the congregation of Fanny Crosby's blindness before they sing "All the Way My Savior Leads Me." To learn that Girolamo Savonarola, author of "Jesus, Refuge of the Weary," eventually met a martyr's death is to add deep meaning to the words of that fine Passion hymn. And what a surprise it is to realize that the author of "Come Ye Faithful, Raise the Strain" is none other than John of Damascus (A.D. 696–754). Imagine how he'd feel to hear his hymn used every Easter some twelve hundred years later.

But that's the beauty of music ministry. To borrow a phrase, "it's a gift that keeps on giving." Creativity flows when music ministry is planned. I believe spontaneity is the result of planning rather than a haphazard jump. To wait for "any favorites" or "the Spirit to move" is to miss out on the creative discovery that comes through the discipline of preparation. This isn't to dismiss those unplanned moments of elation that grace worship, but even Paul the apostle had to caution the Corinthian church that all spontaneity wasn't necessarily spiritual.

This leads to the next area of music and worship.

Performance

We live in a performance-oriented culture. The better we impress people, the louder the applause. No wonder church musicians sometimes try to imitate those who impress people best.

Worship, however, seeks to honor God, not people. The more we understand this, the more authentic will be our music ministry. Here pastors can lead by encouragement and example.

Usually, at the beginning of the fall season I visit the choir at a rehearsal and thank them for their dedication. I remind them of their importance to the ministry of the church. From the very moment of entrance they are observed and emulated by the rest of the congregation.

I tell them of the first time I saw a Norm Johnson choir enter the sanctuary. Every member immediately bowed his or her head in genuine prayer. There was no looking around or talking to each other. Their entire posture suggested meditation and preparation. Most of the congregation bowed with them in humble expectation.

Performance, I tell them, is first to God. Therefore, all their hard work and sacrifice will be worth the effort. I even throw in a little C. S. Lewis opinion that it's better to abolish all church music than to abolish the difficult work of a trained choir.

Then I pray for them at rehearsal and usually on the following Sunday morning in worship. How they perform! But it's unto the Lord. And it's contagious.

What about "special music"? First and foremost, it too is a musical offering. Almost every church has some people who have musical gifts. These good folks need to be encouraged and equipped. Working with the minister of music, pastors can formulate a policy that helps musicians lead worship. Selected well in advance, these people may need help in music choice, spiritual preparation, even appearance.

To sing or play well in corporate worship can be a part of one's spiritual growth. I was interested in a recent quote by well-known conductor Lukas Foss: "If a performer feels he gains a sense of identity in a work, then he will want to play it again." Apparently, the making of music especially unto the Lord can be both a pleasing offering and a powerful spiritual formation.

But a perennial question arises: Which is more important, the quality of the music or the intent of the person? Every church has people who feel convinced of a call to music ministry, while the rest of the church (including the pastor, at whose door the buck stops) feels otherwise.

There is no hard and fast rule, but if a final decision is needed, I put people over performance. While always striving for excellence and encouraging people to do the same, we need to realize that even the finest musical offering by the greatest musician is paltry to the Almighty. Do we dare presume we can add to his musical appreciation or impress him with our melodic expertise? To borrow an incarnation analogy from C. S. Lewis, slugs may make great music for other slugs, but most humans aren't too impressed. God loves music, but his Son lived among, taught, healed, died, and rose again for people. Music is like any other ministry. It is people.

When author Madeleine L'Engle first started attending the village church near her Crosswicks country home in Connecticut, she found herself volunteering to organize and direct a long-dormant choir. She writes in *A Circle of Quiet*, "Some of them couldn't stay in tune and pulled the whole group down into a flat, sodden mass. One woman stayed in key, all right, but at full volume at all times, and with an unpleasant, nasal whine. If the choir was to be a success, the obvious first thing to do was to ease out some of the problem voices.

"But I couldn't do it. I don't know why, but something told me that every single person in that choir was more important than the music. 'But the music is going to be terrible,' I wailed to this invisible voice. 'That doesn't matter. That's not the reason for this choir.' I didn't ask what was, but struggled along. The extraordinary, lovely thing was that the music got to be pretty good, far better, I am now convinced, than it would have been if I'd put the music first and people second."[3]

Purpose informs planning, which then shapes performance. If a pastor is so directed, the music ministry of the church will follow. When I smile and sing heartily during a hymn (rather than thumb through my sermon notes), the congregation sings much better. When I become absorbed in the choir anthem (instead of talking to an associate on the platform), I notice the congregation paying rapt attention. My public affirmation and integration of music ministry into the larger worship service pave the way for the congregation to follow.

But if the pastor helps shape music ministry, I've discovered an even greater miracle. Music ministry helps shape the pastor.

On a Sunday morning several years ago, all our choirs were singing together. They filled the platform and spilled into the aisles. I was hidden behind them, but I could see, in the midst of that sea of heads, the silken hair of my two daughters, Megan and Arwen, and my wife, Dixie. First Arwen's choir, the youngest, started singing, "I love you, Lord, and I lift my voice, to worship you; O my soul, rejoice."

Then the Good News Singers, Megan's choir, joined in: "Take joy, my King, in what you hear; may it be a sweet, sweet sound in your ear." The junior high and senior high choirs blended their voices.

Finally the adult choir entered this musical gift to God, and the entire congregation seemed transformed. There I was, the preoccupied pastor, completely hidden from view, while beautiful children and adults, including my own family, led me to the throne of grace.

With a trembling smile on his face, one very tired pastor caught a radiant glimpse of a heavenly worship yet to come. I knew right then that everything else would be preparation for that Day. And I can't wait to face the music.

---

1. Austin Lovelace and William Rice, *Music and Worship in the Church* (Nashville: Abingdon, 1976), p. 24.
2. Lovelace and Rice, p. 28.
3. Madeleine L'Engle, *A Circle of Quiet* (New York: Farrar, Straus & Giroux, 1972), p. 35.

MUSIC IN TEACHING AND HEALING

Garth Bolinder

I t was the first time I'd ever been to Chautauqua, the historic conference center in western New York. As the congregation gathered in the open auditorium singing "Day Is Dying in the West," I seemed to step back into an earlier era of revival fervor.

Much to my delight, the vespers service was to be a *Messiah* sing-along. I looked forward to singing to my heart's content. Who cared if it was the middle of July?

My first dilemma was where to sit. I can't sing quite high enough to be a decent tenor, yet my shovel isn't big enough to dig out the deepest bass notes. So I sat exactly in the middle and sang whichever way the wind seemed to be blowing.

To my surprise, there were several others like me. There were even some who sang parts Handel never dreamed of. But we were all there to sing great music regardless.

No doubt many people around the world who have sung the *Messiah* have little, if any, saving faith in the One about whom they have sung. But the words proclaim his truth regardless of the condition of the singer (should I say sinner?). One such man was sitting next to me that night at Chautauqua. He made it clear before we started that he was an agnostic, but he loved to sing the *Messiah*. "Great music," he said. "Speaks to everybody, regardless of belief."

Indeed, I thought, *that's a perceptive statement. It'll even preach.* My reverie was broken by the grand overture of the Chautauqua pipe organ. As we began to sing, my companion really entered in. His entire body sang. Several times I thought the spring would break. After we sang the "Hallelujah Chorus," he said, with the veins on his reddened neck still pulsating and a transparent glow on his face, "That's enough to roll anybody's socks up and down!"

Though I'd never heard it put quite that way, he had it right. Music reaches the depths of human personality in ways mere words never can. William Cowper said,

"Sometimes a light surprises
The Christian while he sings."

If music is a primary vehicle for worship, it also aids and supplements the teaching and healing ministries of the church. Scripture gives ample example of this three-fold relationship. King David was a wise leader who knew the power, place, and peace of music. Everyone is familiar with his majestic psalms of adoration to God. They inspire worship. He even managed to sing and dance before the Lord and his troops as they prepared for or returned home from battle. Did Mac-Arthur, Patton, or Ike ever try that?

Consider also, though, how David taught his people through the effective use of song. Many of his lyrics fairly drip with historical facts, political intrigue, and moral admonition. His songs, like modern-day slogans, etched truth into the minds of Israel. We feel their poignant power today.

Or what about David's tender use of music in healing? Instead of angry rhetoric or hell-bent revenge, David took up his ancient lyre and actually played it to soothe the tormented mind and heart of his self-destructive adversary.

I don't remember reading about such an event in the political arena of our day. But then, I can't remember hearing of it during most church fights, either. Would strumming a few notes quench the darting flames of those "well-intentioned dragons?"

Teaching

Music can ingrain truth in the mind for a lifetime. Though usually thought of as applying only to children, this principle applies to adults as well. And the very same junior high students who wail, moan, and gnash their teeth when given a confirmation memory assignment can turn around and sing the latest popular songs word-perfect.

Almost all children sing Sunday school songs. In fact, almost all children sing, period. It's as we get older that we become self-conscious, inhibited, and dull. Children burst with rhythm, melody, and rhyme. So Sunday school and junior church must have lots of music.

The thousands of Suzuki music students around the world testify to the fact that children can master more music than we estimate. Not only are they able immediately to integrate much of the biblical truth in the songs they sing, but great spiritual seeds are planted that will spring into life at a later date. My oldest daughter's choir director is teaching her fourth- through sixth-graders a new hymn every month. This month it's "Immortal, Invisible, God Only Wise." Imagine that! My earliest memory of that hymn goes back no further than college days. Then my third-grader wants to sing "The Church's One Foundation" or "For All the Saints" or "A Mighty Fortress Is Our God" on the way to school. I'd better learn all the verses.

In our media-saturated society, with wall-to-wall music each new day, these implanted hymns are spiritual dynamite. Edna Hong writes about such an experience in her book *From This Good Ground:* "For children, at least for this child [meaning herself], the Word of God received from the church in the home and the church in the community was like a time capsule that activates the spirit at some future date. . . . Even now, half a century later, the capsulated Word of God explodes in my mind and spirit, and a verse that shed no light for me or on me the first time I heard it—or the tenth—or the twentieth time! suddenly illuminates!"[1]

In our work with children's choirs, we've found the following three principles to be strategic:

1. The church and especially the parents of choir children must be active supporters.

2. Choir should be fun. This may be controversial, because good music demands sacrifice. But few of us will commit to something that's repeatedly boring. This is especially true in our channel-switching culture. Don't get me wrong. These children work hard. But it's all in the context of enjoying God's good gift of music.

3. A children's choir is to be educational, not performance-oriented.

Most any church can do this. With the deluge of children's musicals available with taped accompaniment (at a Christian bookstore, or on loan from another church), a committed person can get together a small group of children and begin teaching songs. Even if the choir doesn't grow into a massive chorale, the children are still learning eternal truths about the Christian faith and life.

They're also learning about Christian community ("How come he gets the solo and not me?").

They're also learning music skills.

There's one more benefit. The children's and youth choirs become a "farm system" to feed the "majors," that is, the adult choirs.

As David Wolper said in an interview about his production of the Los Angeles Olympic ceremonies, "We're going to have lots of music, because music is the United States's gift to the world." Children and young people know this very well. So many of the children's and youth musicals available today are upbeat. It's natural for young people to sing them; memory becomes easier; and Christian truth is taught.

Healing

Kelly was a beautiful four-year-old girl. Her willowy hair and crystalline eyes caused people to turn and look when she was carried into a room. Kelly was severely retarded and a victim of cerebral palsy.

My wife worked as a governess to Kelly one summer, and we both fell in love with her. In the process of each day's therapeutic routines, Dixie began to sit Kelly down at the piano and play and sing simple tunes to her. It was as if a peaceful spell came over the girl. If agitated, she calmed down. If distracted, she began to focus. If afraid, she began to trust again. Little by little, the gift of music began to soothe and sort her palsied mind.

It's no wonder E. Thayer Gaston in the book *Music in Therapy* states that all music therapies agree on three primary principles. I list them with some added pastoral comments:

1. *Music therapy helps to establish or re-establish interpersonal relationships* (koinonia, Christian community; no wonder music has been central to God's called-out people).

2. *Music therapy helps bring about self-esteem.* (We're made in the image of God. Humanness was God's chosen means through which to fully reveal himself.)

3. *Music therapy helps utilize the unique potential of rhythm to energize and bring order.* ("God is a God of order, not confusion," writes Paul. The Christian faith and life are not chaotic and confusing. Rather, Christ makes all things new. "We are ambassadors for Christ, God making his appeal through us.")

Though some Christians have explored this area (for example, singer Ken Medema's work with handicapped children), much remains to be learned. We acknowledge the therapeutic value of music at weddings, funerals, and special events. But do we see each worship service, each choir rehearsal, each Sunday school class, each youth group song time as a means for the healing grace of Christ to be ministered to needy people?

This is what cross-country walker Peter Jenkins discovered at the Mount Zion Baptist Church in Smokey Hollow, Texana, North Carolina. The only white person in an all-black church and wearing what he described as a green neon suit, he felt rather self-conscious and alone. But as the service started and the singing warmed up, he felt a tide of spiritual healing flow through the two-hour service.

"Wave after wave washed through the church and washed the people clean. 'A-man, A-man . . . A-man.' "

Then he writes about watching Pau Pau Oliver singing and shouting in the joy of the Lord. This occurred "when a member of the church was so unself-conscious and so immersed in worshiping God that he stood and began to sway and proclaim loudly, 'Thank you, Jesus,' with deep feeling and sincerity. . . . Leaving church wasn't as easy as it was back in Connecticut, where everyone rushed home to eat or catch a football game on TV. On the way out with Zack, Bruce and Eric, I had to shake more hands than I had in years. I felt charged up for life, and here I thought us white folks held all the stock. I came to live for Sunday while I stayed in Texana."

While the culture and styles may be different, what pastor doesn't long for that unself-consciousness and immersion in worship that Peter experienced. What would we do if everyone in our congregations "lived for Sunday"? Music is a powerful agent of spiritual renewal.

Healing is its divine grace note. I need to see music ministry as integral to the life of any church I pastor or belong to. Music is a powerful means of evangelism, the healing of souls. A man who considered himself the most humanistic psychologist in our town came to personal faith in Jesus Christ not through some great preacher or apologist. He happened to slip into the back row of an evening church service and joined the congregation in singing "Alleluia." During that familiar chorus, he realized his spiritual need, recognized the grace of Christ for the first time, and gave him his life. His wife, standing by his side, experienced the same thing. Music is a mighty witness.

Regardless of ability or taste, music can restore and renew any Christian's dry and weary spirit. Be it radio, recorded, or live, music leads the way to the balm in Gilead.

If music can be an agent of healing, of course, it can also be an agent of destruction. I don't intend to harangue on the evils of some modern music, but I do believe we must ask for discernment and discipline so our personal lives, families, and churches can experience the Lord's restoration and renewal. True music, said Martin Luther, "is hateful to the devil and drives him away."

Music is God's glorious and gracious gift. Through it we worship, teach, heal, and fulfill the calling of Christ to minister. It is used in different ways at different times for very different people. The music ministry of your church is as valuable as that of any more visible church with whom you might be tempted to compare. Be encouraged! Music is a gift that's always available. Its ministry in the church can always improve. That will be no more evident than when we one day hear music as it was intended to be.

I wasn't there, but I've heard the story enough to imagine it. When Norm Johnson finally succumbed to the destructive advance of the fatal A.L.S., he spent his last days in a hospital bed in his living room. Family was near, and friends from church, community, and the music industry visited to encourage him and pray. His faithful wife, Lois, was constantly at his side. One evening, a few days before Christmas, he requested again to hear Handel's *Messiah*. As the music enveloped the quiet living room, Norm entered into eternity.

I have often wondered what happened next. How did Norm respond to the Music he'd been waiting all his life to hear? How would he describe it to someone like me?

First I suppose he would digress to encourage me to keep working hard for solid music ministries. He'd remind me it's a worthy goal. Then he'd probably tell me to appreciate what I have. But I imagine he'd also tell me, with a twinkle in his eye, to get ready. Because I haven't heard anything yet!

1. Edna Hong, *From This Good Ground* (Minneapolis: Augsburg, 1974), p. 70.

PART II
YOUTH

S I X
YOUTH PROGRAM HEADACHES
Tom McKee

What aspect of your church's youth ministry has cost you the most sleep?"

I put this question to several pastors across the country, wanting to know what goes wrong most often. Some of the stories sounded familiar. Others were the stuff of which nightmares are made.

"It was the phone call from an irate parent after a boy with 'punk orange' hair sang a Steve Taylor song in church."

"We had a bus wreck that put four of our high schoolers on the critical list in the hospital. One boy was paralyzed."

"A young man was shot while two high school boys were hunting on a youth mission trip."

"Our church is in the middle of a $5 million dollar lawsuit over an incident with a gun at one of our young-singles retreats."

"I had to pull the plug on a music group performing in our sanctuary at an area youth rally."

"We just fired our youth pastor. This is the fourth youth pastor we have let go in four years."

"I had to explain to our board why our youth pastor had put a $2,000 dollar deposit on a retreat center for a youth camp and then canceled it because not enough people registered for the camp. We lost the $2,000."

As I heard these stories, I was reminded of the best seller by Mark H. McCormack, *What They Don't Teach You at Harvard Business School*. We could entitle this book *Lessons We Didn't Learn in Seminary*. However, just because we have graduated from school we are not finished learning. The pastor must always be a student, eager to learn from those who struggle as well as those who are successful in the church. We develop our style of pastoring primarily from experience, not from books; from living in the church, not in libraries.

But lessons from experience can be costly, as the above war stories indicate. So what can we share with one another? The major problems of youth ministry seem to revolve around six headaches, which make up the following chapters of this book:

Headache One: Where do I find good volunteers to run an effective youth ministry? That issue is by far the key in any size church. If the pastor can find dynamic, successful youth sponsors to make up the youth team, the other problems usually fade away.

Headache Two: How do I keep workers from getting burned out, discouraged, or joining another church? As one pastor said, "I just get a great team recruited and trained, when some key people quit. Then I have to start all over again."

Headache Three: How does the pastor of the *small* church build an effective youth ministry? Can you reach and hold teens without calling a salaried youth pastor?

Headache Four: Larger churches wonder how to find and keep a good youth pastor. The average stay is only eighteen months.[1] Where does the pastor find an effective youth pastor for the amount of money the board will approve who will stay at least five years? Once the person arrives, how do the pastor and youth pastor work as a team and yet keep a line of accountability that is effective?

Headache Five: Vision and administration often do not mix. This tension means finding a balance between being nosey about every detail on the one hand and not showing any concern on the other. How does the pastor encourage the visionary and at the same time retain some control over the direction of the ministry?

Headache Six: How should the pastor handle parents, especially those who call upset about some of the youth activities or because their teens are not involved? Another great concern of the pastor is effective counseling ministry for hurting parents. Many of these parents are single, and the pastor often becomes a surrogate parent.

This book is not intended to be a youth ministry how-to. Instead, it deals with the relationship of the pastor and the youth program. I write as a pastor who spent almost fifteen years in youth ministry before taking my first senior pastorate. I have a great love for youth and am a parent of two teenage boys. Four years ago when we planted a new church, and I saw only three teens in the youth group, I was tempted to jump back into the role of youth pastor again—at the same time I was carrying the load of the pastorate. I realized, of course, that I could not do everything.

But I had to examine the role I should take with the youth as senior pastor. Now we have a youth pastor. Questions remain. What is my role now? I am learning how to deal with my concerns in ways other than direct involvement. From my talks with other pastors, many others struggle with this problem, also.

---

1. Paul Borthwick, "How to Keep a Youth Minister," LEADERSHIP, Winter 1983, p. 75.

SEVEN

RECRUITING THE YOUTH TEAM

Tom McKee

Where can we find good volunteers to sponsor the youth program?

Robert Townsend portrays this dilemma for us: "Probably whenever Sitting Bull, Geronimo, and the other chiefs powwowed, the first topic of conversation was the shortage of Indians. Certainly today, no meeting of the high and the mighty is complete until someone polishes the conventional wisdom: 'Our big trouble today is getting enough good people.' "[1]

Perhaps you identify with the problem of finding enough good people to sponsor an effective and vital youth ministry. Perhaps you inherited (or recruited in a moment of panic) some volunteers you wish you didn't have. Take Stan, for example. Stan loved to work with young people. He was always on hand at every activity—energetic, committed, and enthusiastic. But one night at church, he passed around pictures he had taken of one of the girls in the youth group who had modeled for him out in the woods. Although there was nothing wrong in the pictures themselves, people began to be concerned about the countless hours Stan was spending with girls in the group. His wife complained that she and his two young children never saw him.

What do you do with a Stan? You can tell him to stop taking pictures; you can urge him not to neglect his family. However, his unwise and undiscerning behavior will continue to appear in other forms.

Or what about Randy, a parent who volunteered to work with the teens? On his first Sunday evening as youth sponsor, with fifteen teens in the back of his pickup, he was spinning "donuts" in the parking lot after church on his way to an afterglow.

Or consider John, who would never do anything to keep you awake at night. At times, though, you wished he would, because he needed some life. He loved kids, he prayed for them, and he thought he had the gift of teaching. But his classes were boring, and the young people were constantly making fun of him.

Since none of us wants to spend our time untangling webs and lying awake wondering what crazy thing is going to happen next, we need to take seriously the problems of recruiting volunteer staff. Two problems seem to trouble us all.

First, how do I work with the staff I inherited as a new pastor?

Second, how do I find new people to minister on the youth team?

Working with Inherited Staff

The pastor entering a church has two options. One is to clean house. If the youth staff is fanatically loyal to the former pastor, this may be the best option. Every time the pastor tries to work with the youth leaders, all he hears is "But that's not how Pastor Jones did it."

Many of us are not bold enough to fire our staff the first week in a new church and start fresh. However, it is an option; Bill Stuart used it when he arrived as youth pastor at First Baptist of Modesto, California. He had come with the understanding that all youth workers would be dismissed and he would recruit his own staff.

"I just didn't want to fight with anybody who didn't agree with me," he explains. "I wanted to do it my way."[2]

Bill is a strong leader and is able to use that leadership tactic. Others perhaps use the same method but disguise it in political maneuvers that attempt to avoid hurt feelings.

The other option is to work with the staff already in place. However, if you have a problem like Stan, Randy, or John, it has to be faced. No matter how you approach Stan, it will not be easy, because he is basically immature and shows a lack of spiritual depth. If the teens are attached to him, the problem is compounded, and you are in a no-win situation. You can call it "temporary leave" or "creating a new position for Stan," but in his mind it will be interpreted as "firing."

In this case, the Christian education board of the church made a decision to ask Stan to take a temporary leave of absence to spend more time with his family. Stan became very hostile toward the church and bitter toward his wife. After six months, the CE board had to face the matter again and did not reinstate Stan. Although some young people left the church, Stan did not. He remained and continued to hang around the young people every chance he could.

The church never really did solve this. It learned a valuable lesson: Never recruit on an impulse.

Randy does not present as difficult a problem. He is a parent trying to be a kid again, and he can be confronted on his behavior at face value. Usually, if handled immediately, this will solve the problem. If not, he can become another Stan.

When the pastor talked to Randy up front, man to man, and let him know the sponsors needed to set the example even in areas such as driving, Randy responded beautifully. Of course, not everyone will do so. A smaller person will be defensive and get upset about the confrontation.

But we cannot be afraid of these confrontations. The problem that most of us face is not wanting to hurt feelings, so we ignore these kinds of problems. As a pastor I sometimes have to make painful decisions and ask a few people to step down from ministry. I have never been good at this kind of thing, and it does not always go smoothly. I know that some who were dismissed still think they were wronged; however, for the sake of the group and the ministry it was necessary.

Finding New Staff

Filling vacancies has its hazards as well. How do we find sponsors for that rowdy junior high group? This seems to be a constant struggle; people frequently resign their positions, leaving significant gaps in our ministry team.

Back in the twenties, when little Center College's "Praying Colonels" football team defeated mighty Harvard, Captain "Bo" Macmillan was asked how they did it. He replied, "There were eleven men in every play that Center made!"[3] One superstar cannot make a football team or a youth team, and it is important to consider every position carefully.

The truth is, some have the gift of working with young people, and some do not. The Bible teaches that the Lord has put gifts in the church, and one of our primary responsibilities as pastor is to help people discover these gifts and equip them for the ministry (Eph. 4:11-12). We've all known youth leaders who had about as much rapport with young people as a wounded cobra.

Someone suggested placing a want ad in the church paper that reads:

Wanted: A youth worker for a growing youth group—a real challenge for the right person. Opportunity to become better acquainted with people. Applicant must offer experience as shop worker, educator (all levels, including college), artist, salesman, diplomat, writer, theologian, politician, Boy and Girl Scout leader, minor-league athlete, psychologist, vocational counselor, psychiatrist, funeral director, master of ceremonies, circus clown, missionary, and social worker.

Helpful but not essential: experience as a butcher, baker, cowboy, and Western Union messenger. Must know all about the problems of birth, marriage, and death; must also be conversant with latest theo-

ries and practices in areas like pediatrics, economics, and nuclear science. Right person will hold firm views on every topic but is careful not to upset people who disagree. Must be forthright but flexible. Returns criticism and backbiting with Christian love and forgiveness. Should have outgoing, friendly disposition at all times. Should be a captivating speaker and intent listener. Will pretend he enjoys hearing junior highers talk. Directly responsible for views and conduct to all church members and visitors; not confined to direction or support from any one person. All replies kept confidential. Anyone applying will undergo full investigation to determine sanity.[4]

Is this what it takes to be the successful youth sponsor? If so, we can stop looking now. Yet, to be honest, we often think the best person to work with youth is a tall, good-looking, blond-haired young man who is a cross between Joe Montana and Johnny Carson. And in fact, that is what some churches demand today.

But the truth is that often some of the best youth workers are the most unlikely candidates. We need to forget caricatures and be open to the person of God's choosing.

A Recruiting Strategy

It is important to establish a procedure to help people find their gifts. Whether we are working with a team that was handed to us or recruiting a new team, we should consider several key practices:

Recruit task-oriented teams rather than individuals.

Lyle E. Schaller says, "A growing trend is to create a team of five to ten adults to serve as advisers to the junior high youth group. Instead of asking one adult, or perhaps a husband-wife couple, to be the adult counselors, this approach calls for enlisting a team of perhaps seven adults who will share on some community-building experiences, including training, and who will function as a team in working with the fifteen to twenty-five junior high youth."[5]

Schaller goes on to say that churches using the team system usually discover it is easier to enlist seven volunteers than to find one adult who will carry the whole responsibility alone. The team needs an up-front person who can communicate with teens, someone who has the gift of teaching biblical truth in an enthusiastic manner. If the church is small, you may have only one other person on this team with the gift of helps to take care of behind-the-scenes details—distributing and collecting sports equipment, bringing food for the socials, gathering the odds and ends needed for the games. In the larger church, the team may also have someone who is a good listener, effective in one-to-one discipleship, and someone with the gift of administration to organize activities and social events. But the point is that if people can know their roles on the team, they can function with confidence in their area of responsibility.

Help people on the team know exactly what they are supposed to do.

John, the quiet, dedicated young man mentioned at the beginning of this chapter who loved young people, was an unlikely youth worker. Since he was single, he was available to give evenings and weekends. He was available and dedicated. But he really did not have the gift of teaching and had a hard time relating to the young people. He was so quiet he could not command authority, and the youth group often manipulated him. However, to tell John he could not work with youth would crush his spirit.

His pastor took John on a trip; they spent a week together evaluating his life. During that week, the pastor saw the deep dedication of this young man and his unusual desire to pray. In the many hours they spent in the car they talked about his abilities, and they began to forge a job description to fit him.

Following that week, John was moved into a helping ministry. He took charge of transportation for the group. He provided quiet one-on-one counsel with many guys. (One-on-one, he was great. With more than two, he was at a loss.) John came alive with his new role as part of the youth team. The church had done John a disfavor by assuming that everyone who wants to work with youth should be a teacher.

We cannot take every person in the church on a week-long

trip; however, we need to look carefully at our staff and evaluate their positions. Some pastors do this at leadership retreats. Some do this at youth staff meetings once a year. Others meet with their key leaders for lunch or breakfast.

Write job descriptions and a covenant for ministry.

One of the big problems in the church is that we are too nebulous; we do not communicate in writing what we expect of our youth workers. It is helpful to have the requirements expressed in two documents: the job description (what the volunteer is supposed *to do*), and the covenant for ministry (what the volunteer is supposed *to be* in terms of spiritual maturity and commitment to the job).

Stan had no problem with the job description. He knew he could attend all the meetings, plan games, teach lessons, and do anything else on the sheet. Stan also knew what the other members of the team were supposed to do: John would meet with young people individually for discipleship and arrange for refreshments, Mary would call the girls each week, George would teach the Sunday class.

But Stan was never told what he was supposed to be in the area of spiritual maturity. The guidelines about being an example in his devotional life, his attendance at church, the priority of his family, his relationship with the girls in the group, and his supportive attitude toward the entire ministry of the church were never spelled out.

All this can become legalistic, of course, but it is essential to try to make our expectations clear. Some churches include in their youth worker covenants the Scriptures about elders and deacons (1 Tim. 3); others go into great detail about the lifestyle expected of the youth worker. The point is that at the very beginning of the interview you can outline exactly what kind of commitment the church is asking for. Parachurch groups such as Bible Study Fellowship have taught us a valuable lesson: They demand a high level of commitment from their leaders, and they get it. We do the church an injustice by lowering the standard of commitment.

Publicize volunteer needs in the church.

Often people say to me, "Tom, I didn't know the church needed teachers." The opportunities for ministry need to be constantly presented to the congregation. This may be done through sermons, church newsletter, regular surveys (perhaps annual), new-member classes, Sunday school classes, and special presentations in the services. Recently we devised a page of "Want Ads" that we publish every few months advertising our need for workers. We highlight not only teachers but also ushers, volunteer officer workers, and maintenance workers as needed.

Now this can present real problems when the "Stans" quickly volunteer immediately after you have "fired" them. That is the significance of the next practice:

Interview all prospective workers.

Some time ago a young girl cornered me after a message from Ephesians 4 on being equipped for ministry. She felt called to be a youth worker in our church. I had some reservations about her, but since I had opened my mouth in the sermon, I made an appointment to talk with her about it. I called the session an "interview for ministry" and told her I would be asking questions about her philosophy of ministry, Scripture knowledge, and typical counseling questions teenagers ask.

When I asked Karen what Scriptures she would use to talk to a teenager about assurance of salvation, she didn't have an answer. When I asked what Scriptures she would use to talk to a teenager about sexual temptations, she admitted she did not know very much about the Bible. However, when I asked her what counsel she should give to a fifteen-year-old girl who was pregnant, she suggested several insightful options.

Karen seemed to be a good counselor, loved young people, and showed concern. We went through the Bible helping her to find answers to some of the questions we'd discussed; then I challenged her to enter discipleship with an older woman in the church, from whom she could learn more of these things. After a year she could apply for the position again.

She was disappointed, but she was also encouraged about

being discipled. Instead of being turned down, she was affirmed in her desire and guided toward training.

The hours devoted to implementing these practices consume so much valuable time that we are tempted to take short cuts. However, only by establishing a strong base of leadership will we in the long run be free to minister in other areas.

1. Robert Townsend, *Up the Organization* (New York: Fawcett, 1971), p. 96.
2. Interview, *Wittenburg Door*, August 1971, p. 4.
3. Gaines S. Dobbins, *Learning to Lead* (Nashville: Broadman, 1968), p. 79.
4. Ray Stedman, "The Lord and His Workman," *Discovery Papers* (Palo Alto, Calif.: Peninsula Bible Church), February 24, 1974, p. 1. Adapted.
5. Lyle E. Schaller, *The Parish Paper*, February 1984, p. 1.

EIGHT

EQUIPPING THE YOUTH TEAM

Tom McKee

No pastor would intentionally neglect his newly recruited staff. Yet once the recruiting is done, many turn the new staff loose, breathe a sigh of relief, and assume their job is finished, forgetting the important task of equipping the staff to serve. If the youth team resigns, the pastor is back to chapter one.

One minister was excited about his team. A high school coach and his wife, two college students, and the young carpenter who headed the team were enthusiastic and seemed qualified. But soon the phone rang. Jerry, the coach, was saying he had made a big mistake and needed to resign. He had just evaluated his priorities, and something had to go. Pastor Don knew something was wrong, because two months ago when Jerry was recruited, nothing could have stopped him. What had changed?

Jim, the young carpenter, called the next evening and said he felt the youth group would probably do better under Jerry's leadership than his. He felt unqualified. How could this be? Jim had been faithful for two years and was tremendously effective.

As Don began to ask questions, he finally discovered Jerry had many new ideas but did not know how to implement them. He tended to order kids around like his basketball team at high school. "If you don't make the grade, we can cut you from the squad" was Jerry's style. Jim was experienced with teenagers, but he did not know how to handle Jerry and his aggressive leadership. Being sensitive and not wanting to cause trouble, he felt maybe it was time for a change.

Jim and Jerry illustrate several false assumptions about youth workers. They remind us of Lyle Schaller's story about the conflict between the scientists and engineers designing Apollo spacecraft. The scientists wanted a vehicle free of defects so they could use all available space for scientific equipment. The engineers wanted to use the space for more backup systems, contending the only safe assumption was that something would go wrong. The argument was resolved by asking the astronauts in training. They opted for lots of backup systems![1]

The significance of the story is that assumptions are important. Our assumptions determine how we operate. Some assumptions about equipping and motivating youth teams even sound biblical; however, they are dangerous.

False Assumption #1: People Who Work with Youth Professionally (Teachers, Coaches, etc.) Are the Best Youth Sponsors.

This is a logical assumption. Jerry was a natural; however, he had a hard time making the transition from his basketball team to the youth group. Jerry's experience reminds me of my own when I first entered the ministry. I was twenty-two years old, full of enthusiasm about youth, and had just been called as a youth pastor in a church on California's Monterey Peninsula.

I thought this job would be a cinch. After all, I had been raised in an active youth group, my father was the Christian education director, and I had been a campus leader in my

Christian college. A few months before my appointment, I had directed a successful musical using the most qualified talent in the college. I came into this church thinking I could take the same leadership ability and be a smashing hit with the young people.

After one summer of youth ministry, I was dry. Preparing my first lessons for the high school Bible study convinced me I was not really as interesting as I thought I was. When I directed my first youth musical, it was a flop. People did not show up for rehearsals, and I soon realized the caliber of talent in our small youth group was very different than that of the college.

Discouraged, I called my father for help. He gave me the names of two youth pastors in the area and told me to see them right away. Dick and Bob each spent significant time with me and allowed me to watch them in action. I asked questions, observed, and took new enthusiasm and insight back to my group.

I often go back to that experience when I see new sponsors take on a group they have never worked with before. Their initial enthusiasm frequently fades in the first month. We owe it to new workers to provide times of in-service training; we also need to urge them to link up with experienced people both in our churches and others nearby. High school teachers, coaches, and enthusiastic leaders from Christian colleges have great potential, but we cannot assume they will automatically be successful. Working with the typical youth group is very different than the teacher's captive audience or the college leader's talented, mature group.

Nor should we assume that just because they are professionals with youth, they even want to work with youth in the church. Often high school teachers tell me, "I'm with high school students all week long. I don't want to be with them in the church. I would rather minister to some other age group." We load on unnecessary guilt when we assume that just because they teach high school, they should sponsor the youth group.

False Assumption #2: Since the Pastor's Job Is to Equip the Saints, That Means Training the Youth Team Directly (especially if the pastor is a former youth pastor).

Who will sit down with Jerry and train him? I don't have the time to train every leader in the church. I cannot run the youth workshops I used to teach when I was in youth ministry.

However, I can make sure they are trained. I can arrange for them to go to seminars. Most denominations and publishers offer training materials. And most metropolitan areas have Sunday school conventions, with special sessions for youth workers. Workshop leaders in these groups usually love to spend time with enthusiastic sponsors.

Some churches appoint new members of the youth team and assign them as helpers for the first few months. Jerry would be assigned to work with Jim and observe him in action. Jerry would have limited responsibilities at first. The use of teams already mentioned in the previous chapter is a natural for this kind of training.

We can also supply our workers with inspirational reading about youth and youth ministry. Many times I have visited the local Christian bookstore with a youth worker to look at everything from books about teen problems today to "how-to-work-with-teens" manuals to Bible studies and materials written especially for young people. Two resources were invaluable to me in youth work and may warrant your special attention. *Campus Life* is an excellent magazine designed for young people. I found that it appealed to non-Christians as well as Christians. Not only is it good for sharing with teens, but it also gives youth workers insight into the problems of youth and illustrations to use in teaching and counseling. The other resource is *Ideas*, the publication of Youth Specialties in San Diego that contains practical help for youth meetings (crowd breakers, games, skits, socials, and discussion starters).

Many other resources fill the same needs. We need to be sure to supply our workers with these things.

False Assumption #3: Since the Youth Team Is Working for the Lord, They Don't Need Tangible Incentives.

It sounds so spiritual to say, "The Lord will motivate my team." But that kind of thinking forgets that God uses human instruments. The classic example is Barnabas. He was the one to take John Mark, the quitter, and encourage him back into the ministry.

One of the most neglected ministries in the church is the ministry of affirmation. We forget to praise workers from the pulpit and in private. Those who praise the youth team and write notes of appreciation are likely to keep them. Those who take team workers for granted will lose them, not because they are not spiritual, but because we all get discouraged.

Gordon MacDonald says, "As I look back through my life, I am caused to realize that I am the product of a chain of 'affirmers,' men and women who believed in me, who took time to communicate to me their conviction that God had something in store for me in serving Him. Many times I would have quit, dropped out, if it hadn't been that there was some key person who believed in me."[2]

It does not seem to bother God to offer incentives. In *The Mind Changers*, Em Griffin points out that the writer of Hebrews says the expectation of reward is a condition of faith. "For whoever would draw near to God must believe that he exists and that he rewards those who seek him" (Heb. 11:6).

Griffin goes on to show that business and industry have picked up this idea in their marketing. "One tool company switched from talking about their electric drill to describing what the tool would do for the buyer. They said simply, 'We sell holes.' This makes so much sense that it's hard to believe that we in the church ignore the fact that benefits are what people are waiting to hear. But we often do. We tell them what they should believe or what they ought to do without making any effort to show the advantages that come from God's way. All of us need incentives."[3]

As a pastor, I receive tangible incentives from people in the church. Susie and I have been loaned a home at Lake Tahoe, a camper, and a houseboat at various times. I remember times of great discouragement when someone in the church was sensitive to my need and took us out to dinner. It was a little serendipity that God brought along just when we needed it.

What about our youth teams? Do they ever get these kinds of reinforcement? They also face discouragement. The work of the youth leader who is also holding down a full-time job and keeping a family together may become intolerable. Usually this shows in a negative spirit and a questioning of everything. Soon there comes a resignation—or worse, they keep on but with a negative spirit. Some join another church to avoid the pain of quitting the responsibility.

So many times pastors say we should not give dinners or special recognition to volunteers because they "are doing it for the Lord." I wonder how long these pastors would stay in the ministry if they did not get affirmation. How many volunteer youth workers get to travel to annual conventions at church expense? How many have a public platform each week to communicate what they feel deeply inside? How many get to plan their own schedules, with time for the church, home, and work?

Some churches waive all fees for sponsors at youth group outings. Others go further; they take care of baby-sitting expenses, so the youth retreat becomes a retreat for the sponsors as well as the young people.

Equipping for the Long Haul

Too often our youth team is like the three frogs who found themselves trapped in a large urn of cream. One looked at what appeared to be a hopeless situation and soon sank to the bottom and drowned. Another panicked and began to kick his legs frantically to get out. He soon exhausted himself and sank. The third simply kept kicking methodically, steadily, until the cream turned to butter, and he climbed out.

I have seen all three types of workers in the church. Some volunteer and, after their first experience, quit because of fear. Others dive in with great enthusiasm because the need is so great, but they quickly become exhausted. Others, however, evaluate the problems and move methodically with purpose.

Youth work is hard work, and sometimes you are not sure you are accomplishing anything. Our goal is to equip and motivate a team that does not give up in despair or burn out in exhaustion but makes steady progress in changing teenage lives toward usefulness.

---

1. Lyle Schaller, "Assumptions," *The Parish Paper* (July 1983), p. 1.
2. Gordon and Gail MacDonald, *If Those Who Reach Could Touch* (Chicago: Moody Press, 1984), p. 71.
3. Em Griffin, *The Mind Changers* (Wheaton, Ill.: Tyndale, 1976), pp. 100-101.

NINE

WHEN YOU DON'T HAVE A YOUTH PASTOR

Tom McKee

Can a small church have a successful youth program? When the same few young people look at each other each week in Sunday school, can they possibly match the dynamic quality of eighty or a hundred?

I learned a valuable lesson a few years ago from a small Baptist church in San Bruno, California. The youth sponsor was a high school math teacher named Clell. He and his students traveled forty miles to meet with me about a special one-week outreach. They asked me to come speak and bring a seven-member musical group.

When we arrived some months later, I was amazed. About fifteen young people, unified in purpose and direction, had invited their friends. The first night we sang and spoke to about thirty young people; the second night, about fifty came for a night of games. On Thursday night more than a hundred young people came to the church for an all-night volleyball marathon, and a local TV station covered the event.

At the end of each evening, the music group sang and gave testimonies and I spoke. What brought those young people out? I am convinced it was the vision, prayers, and enthusiasm of a small group of teenagers and a math teacher who loved kids. Their unity and spiritual depth was exciting.

From this experience I began to see some things I hadn't realized before:

1. A Small Church Can Think Big.

When I first met with the San Bruno young people to pray, they impressed me with their vision for their peers at school. This group of fifteen, along with their sponsor, wanted to see their friends come to Christ, and they were convinced they could be used by God to reach out. In their prayers they named friends and kept talking about each activity of the week and how it would appeal to kids at school. Not once did they mention they were just a small group and no one would want to attend their meetings. They reminded me of Joshua and Caleb wanting to "take the land."

When we planted Sun River Church in 1980, we had only eight junior and senior high students. But our youth sponsors, Andy and Linda Braio, plunged ahead enthusiastically. They were determined to get involved in the Mexicali Outreach of Azusa Pacific College, which places hundreds of teens in Mexican villages during Easter week. While leading regular activities, they promoted and planned for Mexicali. As a result, our eight-month-old church sent a team of eleven young people and sponsors on a mission to Mexico. The sponsors didn't let being small stop them.

Neither does Lance Mitchell, pastor of a new church in Wilbraham, Massachusetts, which in June 1984 had about fifty members and eighty attending the morning worship service. The youth group went from three to thirty within six months. How? Lance had been discipling a young adult, Barry, who had accepted the Lord through the church. Barry was growing in his Christian life and was taking some video extension courses from a seminary. As he and Lance talked about reaching youth in the town, Barry began to sense God wanted him to leave his managerial position in a department store to work full-time with youth.

Barry presented the idea to the church leaders, and after prayer, they asked him to raise his own salary (similar to the parachurch organization model). In the meantime, they would ask the congregation to foot the bill for the other costs of a three-year pilot program called "Youth Alive Ministries."

The leaders made four initial recommendations to the church:

1. To bring Youth Alive Ministries into existence with a committee and director.

2. To name Barry as director of Youth Alive.

3. To notify their bank that Youth Alive was a subsidiary ministry of the church, and to open its own checking account.

4. To re-evaluate the ministry after three years.

The people of the church got excited. In fact, the first Sunday after voting the Youth Alive into existence, someone put a check into the offering for $12,500. As Lance put it, "We have never received a check for that much before; in fact, I'm not sure any church in New England has received that much in one day for youth work!"

Barry began the ministry immediately and was able to give most of his time to Youth Alive. He supplements his income with some part-time work, such as substitute teaching and officiating at sports events.

Barry is responsible to Lance and the deacons, and is chairman of the Youth Alive Committee. Lance meets weekly with Barry, just as if he were officially on the church staff. Barry tries to disciple the young people he meets, and that includes getting them into a Bible-believing church. However, when Barry is on a campus or at a sporting event, he represents Youth Alive rather than the church.

One of the most successful youth activities was free pizza and pop (called soda in Massachusetts) for the young people after a high school football game. Barry showed the film *Football Fever*, and after his presentation of the gospel, fourteen teens indicated they wanted to make Christ part of their lives. Four of those young people are now attending the church and being discipled.

Four months after beginning the ministry to high schoolers, Youth Alive Junior High began. Now both ministries are steadily growing.

2. A Small Church Can Piggyback on the Resources of a Large Church.

The San Bruno church could not afford a full-time youth pastor. But in essence, they hired a youth pastor for a week. When I spent those days with Clell and the young people, we prayed, laughed, and played together. I also brought seven dedicated, mature young people from my own youth group to provide musical talent, thereby discipling them as well as our hosts. Together we learned how a large church and a small church can work in cooperation.

Many times large churches are looking for places their music groups, drama teams, youth choirs, or evangelistic teams can minister. Some of them would be excited to bring mature college students to counsel for a weekend retreat or help with a special outreach. The small church should be able to find help from these groups.

The first years I was in youth ministry we had a youth choir of fifteen. Many of the large churches in our area, which had youth choirs of sixty to a hundred, put on a youth choir festival every fall. I called the sponsors to see if we could sing in the festival's mass choir. For the first few years we did only that, but when we had grown to thirty singers, we began to do our own special numbers also. The enthusiasm of that all-day festival challenged our small choir toward growth.

Many of the pastors I talked to mentioned monthly skating parties for young people sponsored by the local ministerial association. In Collinsville, Illinois, our local ministerial association had a youth committee that sponsored occasional activities such as concerts for the youth of that city. Many of the smaller churches took advantage of these.

3. The Key to Any Size Youth Group Is the Sponsor.

Not every church can hire even a part-time youth pastor. And, frankly, not every church needs one—if they have a Clell with a burden for young people. In actuality, he was a "tent maker" youth pastor. He taught school for a living, but he was the unpaid professional youth pastor of that church.

But let's be practical; most churches do not have a Clell. One pastor of a small church (about a hundred in Sunday morning attendance and a youth group of about ten) told his experience, which is probably closer to the norm. He and his wife noticed not much was happening in the youth department, so they invited the sponsors over for dinner. They sat around the table and shared ideas. The sponsors then planned several outings (skating, water-skiing) for the next three months.

"As long as I meet with the sponsors every three months and help them plan," he says, "they will do all the work of running the youth program. They just need help getting started." This is no doubt the case in many churches.

4. Communication Is Essential.

How many times has a parent said to me, "You're the pastor—don't you now what's going on in the youth program?" This is a source of real tension for many pastors. They search for the balance between being nosey about every detail on the one hand and not showing any concern on the other.

Some churches make the youth sponsor a member of the Christian education committee, which means giving monthly reports of activities: projects completed and future plans. This is one way for the pastor to stay informed, provided he attends the committee meeting.

Other pastors meet for breakfast or lunch once a month with the head youth sponsor. Others meet for coffee and donuts in the pastor's office once a week at 6:00 a.m. to pray for the concerns of the youth group. This prayer time is a supportive ministry for both pastor and youth sponsor, and it bridges any gap.

5. You Might as Well Start Where You Are.

When you have only three young people in the group, each of them can bring one friend, and the youth sponsor can load them in a car and head for the snow or a nearby amusement park. The most important thing is to be positive about however many teenagers God has sent to your group.

6. It's Crucial to Know Where You're Going.

Two high school boys showed up at my door one evening. They each held huge Bibles under their arms and said, "We want to rap about this book." I was surprised, because I knew them and their reputations. They were absent from school more than they were present.

I invited them in, turned off "Monday Night Football," and listened to their story. They had run away from home, hitch-hiked to Washington, and talked to a pastor, who led them to Christ. He gave them Bibles and told them to look up their pastor and begin studying the Bible. Here they were.

The next Monday they were back with five more young people—of the same type. The next Monday they were back with ten more. In a month we had more than forty young people, all with Bibles, asking me to teach them. They did not want games; they only wanted to study the Bible.

A church down the street was also having a youth meeting the same night. One night when a group walked in late, someone asked them, "Why did you leave that other group?"

I will never forget the answer. A young man said bluntly, "Everytime we go there, they just keep talking about what we need to do to reach the kids of this town. We just keep talking about the same things each week. I like this study because we just study the Bible. We seem to know what we are doing."

The reason that comment was so shocking to me was that I

Don Baker, now pastor of First Evangelical Free Church in Rockford, Illinois, still remembers his first full-time youth minister. Jim joined the staff fresh out of seminary, filled with energy and enthusiasm. He greeted Don the first day with "Hi, Boss—what do you want me to do?"

Baker knew exactly what he wanted, but he did not want to take the time to tell him. After all, he thought, Jim was a seminary graduate; he should already know what needs to be done. So Don told the new youth pastor to go to his office, get on his knees, and ask God.

That is not bad advice; however, it is often a cop-out to avoid personal responsibility. As Baker recalls, "God kept telling Jim to do the dumbest things." And when Baker corrected Jim for not doing what he expected him to do, Baker became painfully aware that he had never really given Jim any direction.[1]

At a youth pastor's conference in southern California a couple of years ago, I talked with dozens of discouraged youth pastors. The word I kept getting from them was "I just wish my pastor would spend time with me. I feel so alone." A few months later I was at a luncheon with a group of pastors who were discussing the problems with staff members. Several of them said, "I just wish he would grab the ball and run. He seems to be floundering, and I don't know how to help him."

Recently a young woman in youth ministry at another church in town sat in my office crying. Full of enthusiasm and talent, liked by the young people, Julie had started her work with high hopes and wanted to "turn the group upside down." But she was defeated and ready to quit after only a few months.

Churches hurt too. One church, for example, has had four youth pastors in the last four years. The church is dynamic, but for some reason they cannot seem to hold a youth pastor, and the young people are beginning to leave the church for another one in town.

How can these problems be prevented or at least minimized? How can we find the right person for youth work? When we have found the proper person, what kind of working relationship should we establish? And if we already have an effective youth pastor, how can we keep him?

Calling the Youth Pastor

There's more than one place to look for candidates to lead the youth ministry. Many churches fail to check out their own congregation. I had lunch with a pastor recently who was looking for a pastor for college students. "We need someone who will not only keep the program going but will really carve out a unique ministry and penetrate the college campuses," he said. Then he told about a Bible teacher in a local Christian high school who was currently heading up the group. "I'm so afraid that this dynamic leader will get a better teaching job somewhere else, and we will lose him."

As he spoke, he stopped. A light went on in his head. "Why didn't I think of it before? He would be a perfect candidate for the position. I think I'll call him tonight."

Or the potential youth pastor may be someone who was once in your church. One of the greatest thrills in my life came when I was called to serve my home church in Los Gatos, California, as youth pastor. To the older people there, I was still Tommy. They saw me baptized when I was seven, watched me grow up, watched my hopped-up '36 Ford roar in and out of the parking lot (some were against my coming on the church staff because they had good memories). But I spent seven years ministering to the youth of my home church after Bible school before going to seminary, and some of those who voted against my call became my most ardent supporters.

My firm conviction is that often we can find excellent staff members in our own churches. Our children's director, Peggy Dorei, and our youth pastor, Paul Thome, are from our congregation. One of the biggest problems I have with reading résumés is that many people look good on paper. The same problem applies to interviews. Most pastors know how to sell themselves, and they do a great job with pulpit committees. Youth pastors are no exception. But when you call someone from your own church, you already know the weaknesses and strengths. You know how the person works with others and with teens.

But this is not always possible. You may not have anyone in your church who would fit the bill, so you begin to search outside.

We wrote to seminaries, denomination leaders, fellow pastors, and asked our congregation to supply us with prospects. We then collected résumés, sent out forms to references, and followed up likely candidates with extensive phone calls to them and their references. During a salary discussion one time an elder said to me, "I want to make sure this person gets enough, because I sure don't want to go through this process again!" Granted, to follow all the procedures and then be turned down—or turn someone down—is discouraging.

One pastor doesn't write the job description until he has a particular person in mind. He looks for someone who can communicate with young people and would be in harmony with the philosophy of ministry of the church. He evaluates that person's gifts. *Then* he writes the job description. If he finds someone with a strong music background, the youth program will definitely have that emphasis. If he finds someone with a strong athletic background, the youth ministry will utilize that tool. This method is reported to be effective.

I have not used that approach. I write the job description, then look for the person who fits. This, too, has proved effective. When we were looking for a youth pastor, we also had some musical needs in the church. I wanted someone who would be able to help lead one of our worship services. We interviewed a lot of young men who would have made great youth pastors, but we did not call them because they did not fill the other need. We waited a long time to get the person we wanted. Paul has now been with us more than three years. He leads the first worship service and has developed a very significant ministry outside of his very effective youth ministry.

When we interview a prospective staff member, five different groups in the church participate. I attend all of the interviews and keep injecting case examples: "What would you do if . . . ?" I even try a little confrontation. I try to point out things that did not go well in the interviews so I can see how the person responds to confrontation.

This takes time, but it pays off. We spent a year and a half looking for our last staff member, but he was worth waiting for.

I personally enjoy working with those right out of seminary and training them. I like spending time with staff, talking about ideas, helping them write goals. That's why I look first of all for people I enjoy and, secondly, for those with whom I sense I can share openly.

In contacting potential youth pastors, I've found it is important to give as much information as possible. When I was graduating from seminary, the First Baptist Church in Collinsville, Illinois, sent me an impressive packet with a profile of the church and information about the town, including maps, brochures, and clippings from the Chamber of Commerce.

When I finished reading all that, I felt I had a pretty good perspective on the church. The last paragraph of the letter mentioned the pulpit committee chairman would be calling me in a week to see if I was interested and if I had any questions. I wrote a pageful, and that telephone call began a very positive relationship. Little wonder I decided to go there.

Managing the Youth Pastor

"I don't like surprises," I often tell my staff. "I want to know what is happening." I guess this goes back to the phone call I got from a parent saying, "Tom, did you know the kids are planning to paint their Sunday school room?" I desperately wanted to answer, "Yes, in fact, the board knows all about it, and we bought the paint!"

Good communication between the pastor and youth pastor can solve major conflict. David Sarnoff of RCA has said, "The power to communicate is the power to lead. . . . Good communication, not structure, is the cement that holds any organization together."[2]

I believe communication is the *major* problem in staff relationships. I have learned not to assume anything but to keep asking questions and be aware of all I can. The problem is, a great deal of friction can develop in this. The following four ingredients provide good lubrication.

The Weekly Written Report. While in seminary I was on the part-time staff of Galilee Baptist Church, Denver, Colorado. Pastor Bob Frederich required weekly answers on paper to six simple questions. At first I resisted. I had worked in successful staff positions for ten years and was a self-motivated, goal-oriented person. Why did I need to fill out these reports? However, since it was part of the job, I complied.

Within two months I was convinced of the value of the procedure. Controversy began to surround my plans for a youth choir tour. As Bob began to answer questions, he had all the information he needed on my staff reports. He knew what was happening before the calls came. He defended my position. I began to realize what an asset it was to have a pastor running interference for me.

I use the same form with my staff today. The six questions are:

1. What significant decisions have you (or your committees) made this week?

2. What significant discipleship experiences have you had this week?

3. What projects have you completed?

4. What projects are in the planning stage?

5. What problems are you facing in your ministry?

6. What personal problems are you facing in your ministry?

Sometimes a question can be left blank. I don't want the staff taking a lot of time to fill this out.

But it is from these reports that I make the agenda for individual meetings with staffers. Sometimes these meetings run only ten minutes; at other times they go more than an hour. Anytime a staff member writes something for the last two questions, we talk about it.

I talked with one pastor who uses a similar approach but without the written report. He discusses three areas at weekly staff meetings:

1. Personal. "How are things at home? How are you feeling about your ministry? Your workload?"

2. The calendar. This opens up all the areas of program.

3. People. They discuss sponsors, youth leaders, elders, and those people in the church they are discipling.

Monthly Relational Meetings. The second ingredient to nonthreatening communication is a monthly meeting with each staff person. I take Paul, our youth pastor, out to lunch, and although we go over the weekly staff report, the conversation is more often a time to laugh and just talk about anything that comes up—books we are reading, issues of the day, theological questions, personal needs. I look forward to these times. Since I have selected staff people I enjoy, these luncheons are a bright spot in my month.

Lillian Toms, pastor's wife at Arcade Baptist Church in

Sacramento, California, does the same thing with staff pastors' wives. She has a regular lunch with the wives in a home. Our staff and their spouses have a fall retreat each year and a social gathering several times a year. It is easy to get so involved in our own ministries that we do not make relational and social time together a priority.

Owning One's Goals. How do I get the staff to perform to their greatest potential? How do I evaluate them without threatening them? By making sure their goals are *theirs*, not just mine.

Julie, the youth pastor who came to see me, was frustrated because she did not know how to put her ideas into action. She had potential and always seemed to be just around the corner from progress, but nothing ever happened. And her pastor didn't seem to know how to help her.

Leadership must liberate people and, at the same time, provide guidelines for productivity. Julie told me that when she was really down, she had gone back to her college pastor from her former church and asked him what to do. He helped her evaluate first of all the needs of the youth group. They sat down together and wrote out the needs, followed by measurable goals to meet those needs.

But he pushed her one step further, which was the key. He asked her to write down three things that she could do *that week* to begin to accomplish those goals. She was to report back the next week. Julie told me that when she saw it on paper, she became so motivated she not only did the three things but "did forty other tasks along the way" (again, her natural enthusiasm shows in her overstatement).

Julie was in desperate need of two things. First of all, she needed accountability. It is sad that she had to go back to her college pastor to find this. Second, she needed someone to help her outline the job to be done.

I require my staff to turn in six-month goals, written in three steps:

1. *What are the felt needs of the ministry?* In 99 percent of the cases, they know exactly what needs to happen. One year, for

example, Paul said he was really concerned about the lack of personal one-to-one discipleship in our high school department. That was indeed the major thing to correct in the next six months.

2. *What are your measurable goals to meet these needs?* Paul decided to train disciplers to work with the high school youth. His measurable goal for the next six months was to recruit and train at least four—two men and two women. (Of course, this was just one of his goals; others dealt with other aspects of the high school, junior high, and college ministries, plus his personal life.)

3. *How are you going to accomplish these goals?*

This is the step often left out, yet I think it is essential for accomplishing anything. Paul set up a summer training program for college-age people to learn how to disciple. He met with them twice a week and taught them principles of personal Bible study and of teaching. Out of that group some of Paul's key disciplers have emerged.

When we recently brought Dave Shelley on our staff, I wrote his first six-month goals. I told him he would be the quarterback of the team in the music/worship ministry. But for the first six months, I would be a play-calling coach. At the end of that time, I wanted him to begin to call his own plays.

As part of the team, I also write my goals and share them with the staff. I want to be accountable to them as much as they are to me. We write these goals in January and early summer. Because we each write our own, we own them; they are ours. It is not a case of the board or the church or the pastor telling anyone what to do. We sense the Lord is telling us what to do as we evaluate our various ministries.

Six-Month Evaluation. The last part of nonthreatening communication is evaluation. Is that a paradox? Can any evaluation be nonthreatening?

Recently I heard about a man who decided to fire an employee. This was his first time to let someone go, and he didn't know how to go about it. So he called the person into his office and asked, "How do you feel about your work?"

By the time the employee finished talking, the boss had given him a raise!

But that did not solve the problem. Without any system of evaluation, the worker had no criteria for improvement. Therefore, there was no change, and he was fired anyway.

I have found that the best criteria for evaluation are the short-term goals each staff person has written. When I meet with a staff member for the six-month evaluation of ministry, we go over these goals. How many were realistic? How many were accomplished? How many are still in the planning stage?

What makes this nonthreatening is that the evaluation measures whether they have accomplished *their* goals. This helps the members of the staff improve and grow in the ministry. Our goal is not to fire everyone who does not reach a standard but rather to help each person become more effective.

Keeping the Youth Pastor

When we have done our homework in calling the right person and following the steps of communication, work becomes a pleasure. A church staff is much like a marriage. It takes a lot of work to be successful, and you don't want to see it break up. I want to keep my staff, and I have found I am more likely to do that if I make sure they are affirmed in the following areas:

Public Affirmation. If the youth pastor has preaching potential, he needs the opportunity to preach. I am thankful my senior pastor allowed me to preach once a month in the evening service when I was a youth pastor. If youth pastors do not have these gifts, we need to make sure they have some public opportunity to present the youth ministry. This may be in a special service put on by the youth, or a report after retreats, mission trips, camps, or a special outreach. We also need to use every opportunity to mention the youth department and our staff in sermons. This affirmation publicly proclaims to the church that you and the youth pastor are a team.

As I mentioned, our youth pastor, Paul, leads our first morning worship service. This puts him in front of the worshipers, ministering to the entire church, not just the youth. He receives much affirmation from the people in that service. This wider exposure is good for Paul.

Private Affirmation. Many churches have only two staff members, but the younger one feels totally out of the planning of the church. In our church, every staff pastor is a member of the church board, voting on all matters of planning. When we began working on plans for a worship center, we spent time in our staff meetings sharing ideas. I wanted to make sure each person is an important part of the team.

Churches with ten or twelve pastors find it more difficult, I know—but it is not impossible. In 1984 I was inspired by the leadership of Peter Ueberroth, the mastermind behind the Twenty-third Olympic Games. To boost spirits, Ueberroth wore a different uniform each day: a bus driver's suit, a kitchen staffer's whites, a blue-and-gold usher's shirt.[3] When the workers saw him in their uniform, it was an affirmation of their place on the team.

If Ueberroth could take the time to identify with the many volunteer and paid workers on his massive team, we have no excuse.

I constantly look for ways to affirm the staff person's work, especially ways they have helped me. It's all right for a church staff to be a mutual admiration society.

Financial Affirmation. I was talking with a member of our church who works for a credit union that seems to have an unusual record of employee tenure. I asked what was their secret. I learned they had done a comparative salary survey of credit unions across the country, then decided to implement a merit system that put their best employees a step above their competitors. Each individual employee is reviewed regularly, and if they merit an increase, management awards an incentive raise in addition to a cost-of-living raise.

Obviously, other credit unions have not been able to steal their best workers. Of course there are other considerations beside salary in keeping an employee; however, we should never minimize the financial aspect. Each year I try to research what other churches are paying and pass this information along to the board so they can carefully consider the salary of each staff member.

Perks. Many pastors plan mission tours or trips to the Holy Land, but the youth pastor rarely has this opportunity. Why not? When I was in my sixth year in Los Gatos, I got to lead a youth mission team to Europe for a month. What a privilege!

Some churches offer study leave or sabbaticals. Many times a youth pastor is burned out after five years, and a month off to study or a mission tour would do more for him than a change of churches. Sending a youth pastor and his wife to youth worker conventions is a wise investment, another of the perquisites that encourages a team member.

Many pastors say, "I'm weak on administration—that just isn't my gift." Even so, if they are going to lead a church staff, they must learn the principles of calling, managing, and affirming. We can all grow to become not only adequate but successful church executives.

---

1. Don Baker, *Leadership* (Portland: Multnomah, 1983), p. 3.
2. Ibid., p. 14.
3. "Man of the Year—Master of the Games," *Time*, January 7, 1985, p. 38.

ROADBLOCKS AND GUARDRAILS FOR VISIONARIES

Tom McKee

I love visionaries, and Nick was a visionary. In fact, Nick's enthusiasm and love for the Lord were contagious; he was a great impetus to the vision of the church. But Nick was coming up with a different idea each week.

One week he walked into my office with an idea how we could reach all the Vietnamese refugees in our city. Two weeks later he was wanting to sponsor a World Vision hunger campaign with our young people. The next week he was ready to take a group to Haiti to help construct a hospital. Nick wanted to do it all, and in fact, many of his programs were effective. But he burned out many people in the process and rolled over anyone who did not agree with him—including me.

The term *administration* is a confining word for a visionary; it seems to limit the Holy Spirit. Visionaries prefer spontaneity and allowing the Holy Spirit to lead. They say too much administration hinders the Spirit and limits the vision of the church. In short, they consider *administration* and *vision* contradictory.

It is refreshing to work with someone who wants to move.

But with two or three visionaries like Nick, the church can become spastic—jerking and groping this way and that without any real direction.

How do you manage a visionary? How much freedom do we give the youth group, for instance, to have its own dreams and then act on them? How do we allow other groups in the church to have their own authority for making decisions without creating church-splitting issues?

This tension reminds me of the faculty member who told his colleagues in a leading university, "The state legislature has always granted us complete academic freedom here, and if we don't do what they want, they are going to take it away from us."

Pastors stand in the middle of a tension. We want visionaries to make decisions and carry them out; on the other hand, we want to have some sense of control. Our fears of either too much or too little control often cause us to set up unconscious roadblocks that hinder the work of the Holy Spirit and limit our visionaries.

In order to allow both freedom to experience the gifts of the Spirit through the visions of our people and to establish some guidelines to keep our direction sure, I've discovered two roadblocks that must be eliminated and two guardrails that must be erected.

Roadblock 1: My Way Is Best

Being a former youth pastor has its benefits. I get to speak at occasional youth meetings; people respect my experience and ask for my advice. There is, however, one major drawback: I have to keep reminding myself that the way I did it may not be the best way.

There have been times when our youth sponsors have an idea that, because of my vast experience, I know will fail. I don't want to discourage them when they are so excited, and because I know we learn through failures, I grant them my blessing. Many times, however, much to my surprise, they see fantastic success.

One example is the way young people report back to the church after a camp or mission experience. I had some terrible experiences with spontaneous reports from teens. One young person told the congregation about driving down the highway at high speeds and how "God had protected them" (I am constantly amazed at the "blessings" credited to the Lord). We had an interesting deacons meeting after that testimony time. Strict rules were imposed on the youth group, though I felt them unnecessary because I knew the incidents had been greatly exaggerated.

As a result of that experience, I became very careful about services when young people would report back. I appointed the individuals who would share and gave each of them a subject. I coached them in their presentation. The next sharing time was dynamic. People left the church service uplifted and moved. What a difference from the previous experience! I called it a success and drew the conclusion that "organized sharing" was the only way to go.

Now, ten years later, I am still running scared when young people speak. But when I imposed my feelings on our youth sponsors and told them to pick certain young people to share and assign them subjects, the sharing was stiff and artificial. As I listened, I saw my own over-reaction to a situation. I had to swallow my fear and tell the youth sponsors they were right and needed to let the young people share more spontaneously, like they wanted to. The next sharing time was great—and without any horrendous stories.

There are also tremendous differences from church to church, from group to group. What works in one church may not fit in another. Sometimes even within the same church, what works one year may not work the next. I often forget that and start telling people what worked for me, assuming it will work for them. The way I did it is not necessarily the best, even if it worked once. Things may be different now. Visionaries must be given permission to try new things—and even some old things over again.

Roadblock 2: Decisions Come from the Top

As a youth minister, I experienced one of the most dramatic changes in a group I have ever seen. It began with about twenty high schoolers who met with their sponsors to pray and plan for the coming year.

Our group was in limbo. We had an active program—Sunday school had over 200 attending, youth choir around 100, Tuesday morning discipleship training about 100, Wednesday night prayer meeting about 30, and monthly socials with anywhere from 50 to 200, depending on the activity. On the outside it looked fine, and most of the young people enjoyed coming. But something was wrong.

There was no fire. Few young people were being changed. Even fewer were making an impact on campuses. Most were just living quiet lives of going to school, attending activities, and living at home.

I was concerned but did not know what to do. How do you turn a stationary ship? And even if I knew *how* to change it, I was not sure what direction I would go. People were coming to me from all over the state to see our youth group, but I felt it was stale. There must be more.

We began to ask ourselves hard questions about our ministry, and before the evening was over we had a new vision of what needed to be done, and it was the group's vision — not mine alone.

Our young people decided they wanted to drop Wednesday night prayer meeting and begin an outreach ministry called "Breakaway" on that night. My job was then to present this idea to our senior pastor. I have to admit I was afraid to go and tell him the young people wanted to drop prayer meeting. We were a Conservative Baptist church, and the idea of not having a prayer meeting on Wednesday evening seemed radical. I had been in the church as long as I could remember, and at times I thought midweek prayer meeting was one of Paul's instructions to the church.

We were also proposing a change in the unwritten dress code. Girls always wore dresses to prayer meeting, but since they were going to sit on the floor, we were telling the young people to come in jeans. In 1968, that was radical! Anxiously, I made an appointment with our pastor.

I was floored when he said, "That's what we need around here — some enthusiasm from people who really want to reach out beyond our walls! Let's go for it!"

How grateful I am for the lesson I learned from my pastor: Initiative doesn't have to come from the top. I am so thankful for a pastor who allowed us to make decisions and follow through. He knew the group that initiates has the vision, and he knew that if the group was constantly hemmed in, they soon would lose all vision.

With the support of the pastor and board, Breakaway took off, growing in its outreach until two hundred to three hundred young people would crowd the church each Wednesday evening.

An interesting footnote: In about three years, Breakaway died. The twenty young people who had prayed and planned Breakaway into existence all graduated, and those left in the group did not have the same vision. To them, Breakaway was a program that had been handed down. I had a hard time trying to excite the new group to the old group's vision. They needed to pray and seek God for a vision that was their own.

I don't think of myself as traditional; however, I have to admit at times I am. Since so many foundations are being shaken in our society, I do find security in some traditional programs that offer permanence and security. But I'm also learning to allow freedom. Now, from the pastor's viewpoint, I'm learning to eliminate that second roadblock.

This, however, raises perhaps the most complex problem. We need an atmosphere of freedom to spark vision, but where do we draw the line? How do we keep the fire of enthusiasm from raging out of control? Too many ideas, even good ideas, leads to anarchy. How do we harness the energy of a visionary? We need a few guidelines — guardrails —to point our visionaries in the right direction.

Why We Need Guardrails

When working with an enthusiastic visionary, we must remember that not every vision is God's plan for our church. It took me years to learn this principle, but when I did, I was liberated from the tyranny of following everyone with a conviction.

I often think of the story about the farmer who got up in the morning to feed the sheep. He started to get the feed when he saw the tractor needed to be fixed. He started for the barn to get the tools when he saw that the wood needed to be chopped. He started to the wood pile to get the ax when he noticed the horses were out of the corral. He ran to catch the horses and then noticed the barn had caught on fire, so he forgot the horses and ran to put out the fire. While putting out the fire, he heard his wife yelling to him that the gas stove was not working and he needed to fix it.

I feel that way sometimes in the church. I am so busy fixing up everything that I don't have time to feed the sheep, which is what I started out to do in the first place. I see broken programs and broken lives; I run from crisis to crisis and at the end of the day wonder what I have done. Then someone comes up to me with a new vision—which is usually a new broken person or group of people who need fixing. The next thing I know, our church is directionless as I chase from one fix-it project to the next.

I need guardrails to keep me from straying too far off course.

Some years ago, I discovered a helpful metaphor: In many cities the gospel message is preached in many languages, perhaps as many as a hundred. However, there is not one local church that preaches the gospel in every one of those languages. Each unique church has a special calling of God for ministry. This was a liberating concept for me personally, because I go to bed at night thinking of much more that could have been done and more people who could be reached. And when I had listened to visionaries like Nick, I struggled between guilt and fatigue. However, I began to realize that as a church we cannot meet every need. Churches each have a different "language."

So how do we know which visions from our people are from the Lord? How do we know in what language we are to be preaching? How do we know just what specifically we are to do? I have two guardrails that help keep me on course.

Guardrail 1: A Philosophy of Ministry

One of the most important aspects of ministry for a pastor is to help each church develop a philosophy of ministry. This states the direction the church takes on certain issues. This style of ministry—this "language"—is what distinguishes it from the other churches in town.

Recently a mother walked into my office with a tape she had just heard. She was convinced that the Lord had directed her to this tape and the lecture by a youth pastor about the evils of rock music. She told me about the lecture and all the satanic messages in rock music. If young people would just listen to this tape, she contended, they would burn all their rock music records, including so-called Christian rock music.

I explained to her that if there were those in the church who wanted to listen to the tape and burn their records, that was fine; however, as a church we were not a "crusading congregation." We do not lead negative crusades against such issues; our philosophy of ministry is to preach primarily reconciliation to God. Where the Bible is dogmatic we want to be dogmatic. But when an issue is open to individual interpretation, we want individuals to come to their own conclusions on those matters. There are many churches in town who are very involved in these kinds of crusades, but the elders do not sense that is the direction the Lord is leading Sun River.

This woman had a vision, but the vision was contrary to the direction of the church. When she heard our philosophy, she struggled with our church and since has left.

We have spent time on our elder board working on different issues that come up — the role of women in our congregation, the place of the divorced in ministry, etc. These are not easy issues, and in many cases I am not sure we are correct; however, we say this is the stand we take until Scripture and the Holy Spirit convince us otherwise.

To use the analogy of language, this is the language we preach, and there are many churches in town that preach the message of Christ in different languages. We encourage people to worship where they preach in their language.

This philosophy of ministry must be regularly communicated to the church. Olan Hendrix, in *Management and the Christian Worker*, says the effectiveness of any corporate effort depends largely upon our ability to concisely articulate our objective.

I believe the most effective way to communicate the philosophy is in the sermon. From time to time when a certain issue presents itself in a text, I will mention, "The elders of Sun River have taken a stand on this issue and are leading the church in this direction."

In addition to the sermons, sometimes we devote our evening service to one aspect of the philosophy of ministry. Recently, just before the election, I presented our position on the separation of church and state. Our church would not endorse particular candidates or tell people how they should vote on issues. We would merely encourage people to pray, be informed, and vote.

Our philosophy of ministry is never static. We are constantly growing and being challenged. I hope that never changes, because I would never want our guidelines to become so rigid that they hinder the work of the Holy Spirit. We have to realize the Lord often sends a visionary our way to help us evaluate our philosophy of ministry and get us out of a rut. We need to be careful that we do not cut off our visionaries by having our guidelines too rigid.

To help us evaluate our guidelines, we need our second guardrail.

Guardrail 2: Clear Lines of Communication

In my first pastoral experience, as a summer intern, I made a big mistake. I wanted to attend a concert to hear the musical ensemble from the Christian college I was attending. The concert was on a Wednesday night (I've already mentioned how sacred the midweek services were then), and the college was an hour's drive away. I asked the pastor if I could take the day off and attend the concert, and he gave me permission.

What I did not tell him, however, was that I also asked five young people to go with me. That Wednesday evening when the youth group arrived for prayer meeting, five of the youth group leaders were absent. When people began to ask where these young people were, the answer was "Oh, Tom took them with him to a concert." This not only created jealousy among the young people, but the pastor stood there with egg on his face because he did not know the whole truth of what I was doing.

The next day the pastor and I had a confrontation. I have to admit I was not surprised. In my youth and determination to do it my way, I felt he never would have allowed me to take the young people, so I didn't ask. I just took them and decided to face the consequences later. As they say, it's easier to get forgiveness than permission.

The consequences, however, besides getting "chewed out," were far more significant. I lost credibility with the parents and with my pastor. He was surprised and hurt by my decision, and he explained that I had put him in a tough position. He desperately wanted a youth pastor in the church and wanted the experience of an intern to be successful. I had hindered that vision through my own selfishness. It took time to regain any credibility.

I learned a valuable lesson in communication. Years later when we wanted to start Breakaway and drop Wednesday evening prayer meeting, I knew there were certain lines of communication and accountability I had to follow. I would never have just dropped the prayer meeting without a discussion with my pastor and the board. The lines of communication were not merely a "permission step" but a "support step."

The pastor and deacon board became so excited about Breakaway that they changed the plans on the church's "facility priority list." The deacons were going to remodel an old fireplace room, but it was twentieth on the priority list. They moved it to number one because they caught the vision for Breakaway. They knew we needed a comfortable, warm setting for our ministry and approved the considerable expenditures for the renovation job.

Every church must establish these lines. They can be through the Christian education committee, the church board, or the staff, but these important lines must be used. And when the committees and boards are aware of the philosophy of ministry and the lines of communication, a direction is set to keep our visions on target.

This is not to say that visionaries will not challenge our guidelines; I hope they never stop challenging us. As long as we have an active, ministering church, I can guarantee we will be challenged. That is the nature of a church on fire. But part of the process of growth and maturity is developing and refining these guidelines together.

TWELVE
HELPING PARENTS
IN PAIN
Tom McKee

I watched with two horrified parents as their seventeen-year-old stood on top of her bed holding a butcher knife and screaming at us. The mother was crying; the father was so mad I thought he was going to get a gun. Somehow—I really don't know how, except by the power of God—everyone got calmed down enough to go sit in the living room.

This was not the first time I had been called to actually negotiate peace terms in a home. Sometimes communication *completely* breaks down. Parents are ready to tell their children to leave because of a total disrespect for authority. Teenagers are ready to run away, or perhaps already have.

On the opposite extreme was a mother who called me just before a choir tour. Her daughters were mature, stable Christians, assets to our group. The mother expressed her concern over our planned beach trip while on tour. How would the girls dress on the beach? I could tell she was carefully weighing every word I said, trying to decide whether to allow her girls to go on tour.

She was a concerned parent. She cared about her girls and the youth ministry. Was her concern overprotective or not?

Whether the question centers on an activity (should the group sponsor an all-night party, or a Christian rock concert?) or the influence of certain types of kids attending the youth meetings, the concerned parent will keep your phone ringing. Sometimes this person has failed to get the desired action from the youth sponsor or youth pastor and is trying an end run through you. Still, he or she deserves a hearing and honest consideration of concerns.

Parents are the oft-forgotten team members in youth ministry, the forgotten chapter in books about youth ministry. Frequently we leave them to struggle by themselves in a world where they need input and support. As a matter of fact, we all need each other's support. We are all on the same team, supposed to be going the same direction. And the parent members include a variety of players. Here are some of them:

Parents in Need

Those with a teenager in love. One hundred young people had gathered at 6:00 A.M. on Saturday morning to leave for a week of choir tour. With all of the parents, too, they made a sea of people in the church parking lot. Fourteen-year-old Shelley suddenly came up as we were loading and said she couldn't go, but she had come to say good-by to her friends. She was a quiet girl, and I didn't think anything about it as we loaded suitcases and checked everyone else off. We prayed and left.

A week later, the same group of parents were waiting to welcome us home. Later that evening I got a call from Shelley's parents.

"Tom, was Shelley on tour?"

I panicked as the story began to piece together. Shelley had spent the week camping with her boyfriend. She arrived as the bus came back, however, and greeted her parents normally. The trouble was, one of her friends came up and said, "Boy, did you miss a great trip!" Her scheme was exposed.

Shelley's parents are fine Christian people who have been active in the church. They love their children and want to do right. They were stunned at this behavior as they tried to figure out what to do next.

Many parents have experienced the total change of behavior in a teenager because of a dating relationship. A son or daughter who was showing spiritual growth all of a sudden seems to become a different person.

The single parent. If this book had been written twenty years ago, this paragraph would probably have been missing. But the number of single parents is growing, and they present new concerns to pastors and churches. Somehow we must support the large number of women who are struggling financially, emotionally, and spiritually with their teenagers, and men who feel the terrible pain of a broken family.

Parents with an unresponsive rebel. Every time our young people are given a service in which to testify about a camp or mission experience, an unintentional stress results. The congregation is excited about changes in the lives of these young people—but at the same time, some parents sit in the audience (or stay home) wondering why *their* wayward child does not respond to God's call. I don't think anyone can understand that pain unless you have lived through it.

Dr. John White writes in *Parents in Pain,* "Although I am a practicing psychiatrist, my confidence does not spring from any psychiatric expertise. For I am also a practicing father, one who has made mistakes, who has struggled at times with a sense of hopeless inadequacy and who has grappled with the shame and the pain about one of his five children who went astray. I have known a sickening dread when police cars drew up to my house and men in blue walked up the path to the front door. I have known wakeful nights, rages, bitterness, frustration, shame, futile hopes being shattered and the cruel battle between tenderness and contempt."[1]

As pastors we must do more than be aware of this tension. We must beware of easy answers and quick advice. Frequently we must serve as comforter, listening quietly to broken parents pouring out their heartache.

When a pastor friend of mine went to talk to a well-known

Christian counselor some years ago about this kind of situation, he felt blasted. In just a few minutes the counselor had assessed the situation and began lecturing my friend about his failure to spend enough time with his children when they were young. The pastor and his wife felt more discouraged than ever when they left, angry at the oversimplification of a complex problem, guilty about their failures, and without any new insight or solutions.

This is particularly a danger if the pastoral counselor is younger than the parents and has young children of his own. I love Charlie Shedd's prologue to *Promises to Peter*.

How to Raise Your Children

This was the title of one of my finest efforts. Like all good speeches it had unity, order, movement. It electrified, edified, specified! It grabbed them quick and held them fast with humor, pathos, drama! All over the Midwest I gave it. They paid me a handsome fee and they were glad to get me. "This guy will wow you!" That's what they said, and the people came. With high hopes, they came for "How to Raise Your Children."

Then we had a child!

That sound you just heard was the great elocutionist falling flat on his face. My majestic speech (honest, it *was* great) had been totaled. Those brilliant ideas had such a droll sound at 2:00 A.M. with the baby in full cry!

In my defense I want you to know this—I kept on trying. I changed my title to "Some Suggestions to Parents," and charged bravely on. Then we had two more children and I altered it again. This time it came out "Feeble Hints to Fellow Strugglers."

From there it was all downhill. The appeal was out of it. My drawing power moved to zero. (I forgot to tell you the honoraria went down with each revision.) But for another thing, I couldn't stand to hear me.

So today I seldom speak on parenthood. And whenever I do, after one or two old jokes, you'd catch this uncertain sound . . . "Anyone here got a few words of wisdom?"[2]

In addition to the parents described above, most churches

have overprotective parents, domineering parents, and I-don't-care parents.

The Group Approach

What can we do to encourage and include these people? I have found that one of the most helpful methods is the support group. The beautiful thing is they can be tailored to any situation. For example:

The small impromptu group. Joanne was a pretty, cheerful young girl who showed much promise while in the youth group. She graduated from high school and attended Bible college. During the summer after her first year of school, she met a man who was divorced, not a Christian, and about fifteen years older. Her life radically changed, and in a few short weeks she dropped out of church, lost her smile, and drifted into a lifeless rebellion.

Joanne's mother, Lucy, was a remarkable woman. I have never seen a mother do what she did. Lucy called two close friends, and together they banded together three times a week for an hour of prayer for Joanne. These women wept on their knees for a solid hour in specific prayer.

At first there was no change. Joanne seemed hostile to her family and especially any contact from the church. Anything we tried to do failed—except those prayer meetings.

Within one year, Joanne's life changed. The relationship broke up, and she began to reach out for restoration. The prayer group and the church as a whole loved and sought to restore Joanne.

I have shared that story with many parents whose children are being rebellious, but I have found very few who are willing to give themselves to diligent prayer for the restoration of a child. I believe one of the greatest untapped potentials of a church is prayer. We go to seminars, read books, listen to tapes, join support groups, and complain a lot about our children, but too often we do not pray for them.

The Larger Organized Group. One of the most effective

groups I have been a part of was a parents' prayer meeting during the Sunday school hour. I met for a quarter with parents who were struggling with the typical questions. I, the youth pastor, was the group facilitator, leading the discussion and praying with them.

We found that communicating with each other about curfews, dating standards, music, and current trends became a great help to parents, who so often feel alone. Especially single parents felt that support, and couples often reached out and upheld them in their difficult decisions. But most of all, we learned there were no guarantees. We could not sit around and feel smug that if we did everything right, our children would be model Christians. We realized every child was unique.

When I think of the responsibility of parenting, I am reminded of the story of President Theodore Roosevelt. A friend noted the frenzied behavior of his daughter and asked, "Theodore, isn't there anything you can do to control Alice?"

Roosevelt responded, "I can be president of the United States, or I can control Alice. I cannot do both."

What parent has not felt that tension of responsibility between family and outside commitments? We all need support and encouragement, and we neglect an important aspect of youth ministry if we forget to include the parents of our teenagers.

1. John White, *Parents in Pain* (Downers Grove, Ill.: InterVarsity, 1979), p. 14–15.
2. Charlie Shedd, *Promises to Peter* (Waco, Texas: Word, 1970), p. 7.

T H I R T E E N

C.E. DOESN'T RUN ON AUTOPILOT

John Cionca

After eleven years in Christian education, I became a senior pastor. Previously I had been a specialist — holding C.E. positions in three churches, completing three graduate degrees in education, and serving several Christian and public-school organizations as a consultant. Suddenly I was a general practitioner in a congregation of 250.

As a minister of Christian education, I had always wondered why senior pastors showed so little interest in C.E. Oh, they definitely wanted a strong Sunday school, but when it came to direct involvement, they seemed conspicuously absent.

After six years on the other side of the fence, I've gained a new perspective. The pastor *is* interested in Christian education . . . and missions and counseling and shepherding and stewardship and preaching and . . .

I am still convinced education is a top priority. After all, with Americans now watching an average of six hours of television a day (and in the crucial value-forming years between six and eighteen, the average young person sees 35,000 commercials), I ask myself, *How much exposure to the Word do my people receive?* Looking at many of their lives, I think of the

Lord's words to Hosea: "My people are destroyed from lack of knowledge." My sixty minutes of weekly preaching hardly begin to offset the molding capabilities of the world. Any pastor who thinks he can adequately teach and train disciples alone is likely suffering from a malfunctioning diode.

I can't put Christian education on autopilot and expect it to have significant impact. Even though as senior pastor I have many more responsibilities, I cannot neglect the vital ministry of education.

Resident Chief of Staff

I have changed the way I see my role in the church. I am not a specialist, working with intricate systems and programs. I am not even a general practitioner treating all the patients myself. I am more like a hospital chief of staff. We pastors are the ones primarily responsible for the welfare of those who come to our institution. We are involved in both preventive and curative medicine. We proclaim what people should and should not do if they want to remain healthy. We also meet regularly with the hurting, sometimes even taking them through a spiritual chemotherapy in an attempt to arrest growing cancers.

Important as my function might be, however, I am not the only doctor in the house. The size of the task is beyond any one doctor, or minister. A well-run hospital has a medical staff with expertise in specialized areas. God has not called me, a pastor, to be the only healer; the Great Physician has called me to be a chief of staff.

Our ministry is multiplied as we recognize and develop the team of gifted people the Lord has given to every church who can teach God's Word.

We are all aware that 2 Timothy 2:2 instructs us to pass our knowledge on to others who are faithful and will join us in the teaching process. We have preached from Ephesians 4:11–12 that our task is to prepare God's people for the work of ministry. In 1 Corinthians 12 we have observed even a messed-up church with all the spiritual gifts, implying that each local church has everything it needs for building itself spiritually.

Yet because of deadlines, pressures, and expectations, I was finding over 90 percent of my weekly hours given to "things *I* do" rather than encouraging and helping others who share the ministry of our church.

My sermons, no matter how well developed and delivered, are just not enough. Little Johnny needs the Scripture memorization of the club program; Mary needs the encouragement of the senior high youth leader; Mr. Clark needs the spiritual discoveries he makes at the home Bible study. If we want to maximize learning, we must concentrate on what our lay people are doing.

Here are a few lessons I've learned since trying to become the resident chief of staff.

Look for the Right People

What type of person makes a good teacher? I once heard someone say the best worker is always FAT—Faithful, Available, and Teachable. I now agree.

Working with people, I have become less impressed with background and credentials, and more impressed with attitudes and performance.

He may be a pipefitter or an executive, she may be a lawyer or a homemaker, but the faithful, available, teachable person is able to minister in a deep way to students.

Sometimes we are overly concerned that teachers have a good Bible knowledge before teaching. A friend of mine became a Christian when he was twenty-six years old. Immediately he was encouraged by a pastor to get involved teaching Sunday school. The man began to teach a class of children, and each week he diligently studied the printed teacher's guide to be adequately prepared for his kids. It was not unusual for him to call the pastor's elementary-age daughter to figure out how to pronounce the names of certain Bible personalities or book titles. If you were now to ask Dr. Donald

Orvis, seminary vice-president and professor, what helped him grow spiritually, he would include at the top of the list his early teaching experience where he was just "one step ahead of the pack" each Sunday.

A knowledge of Scripture is important. Maturity is desirable. But the right attitude and demonstrated faithfulness in small ways are the most important characteristics. Obviously, some Christians need more encouragement and closer supervision. Nevertheless, FAT people grow in Bible knowledge faster than others, and working with them in ministry is a joy.

Recruit with Class

If there is an unpardonable sin in teacher recruiting, it's the old trip-them-in-the-hallway trick, where you thrust a Sunday school quarterly into their hands as you pick them up and point them toward the junior department.

We have all learned the hard way that "you get what you pay for." The same principle applies to recruiting. Paint an inadequate picture, tell a prospective worker that the task will not be too hard, and you receive an inadequate, half-committed teacher.

I've used the following plan in recruiting program leaders, and many of them, in turn, are finding it effective in recruiting teachers.

1. Telephone the prospective worker. "Hello, Mary. I've been looking at our church membership list trying to think of someone who could work well in Sunday school with our sixth-grade girls. As I prayed over a number of possibilities, I thought you might be one who could really help our gals. Would it be possible for us to meet this weekend to discuss the responsibilities of the sixth-grade worker? If you are like I was a few years ago, perhaps you have some doubts. But I would really like to have an opportunity to chat with you about it, and then allow you enough time to think about it on your own. I have Saturday morning at 10 o'clock and Sunday afternoon at 4 o'clock open on my schedule. Would either of these times be convenient for you?"

2. Share the importance of the program. I walk through the details of the job description (see sample) and explain the materials. It's also important to stress my availability as a resource to the teacher.

Then, as I prepare to leave, a prayer is appropriate. I encourage the prospect to pray about this opportunity during the week—is this invitation God's call?

3. Make a follow-up phone call five to seven days later to see what questions the person might have and to see if he or she is interested in observing a few class sessions.

4. If the worker is willing to teach, we set up a time to sign an Annual Appointment to Service—a one-year teaching contract (see sample). Materials are further explained, and the new worker is told the time and place of the next department staff meeting.

5. If certain individuals are not able to make the commitment, I try to determine if they would be more comfortable as a substitute teacher or if they have an interest in another area of ministry.

We recruit teachers to serve one year. Shorter terms do not allow workers to assume ownership of the position. The time is insufficient for training, and it is unfair to the students. On the other hand, placing someone in a position indefinitely is unfair to the worker. At the end of each yearly appointment, the teachers have three options: (1) turn in their materials and be finished with their responsibility, (2) sign on for another term of service in the same area of responsibility, or (3) request a change in ministry.

Our experience has been that teachers who have been regularly encouraged have been more than happy to renew their commitments year after year.

Communicate Regularly

A year ago when our church began two morning worship services and two hours of Sunday school, we did a poor job of communicating. Some of the teachers didn't find out which hour they were teaching until the assignments were printed in the church newsletter in July. They hadn't been consulted, and some of them felt taken for granted.

We should have called a faculty meeting to present our options and let the teachers point out any problems or oversights.

This fall we did much better, even though the assignments weren't made until August. We informed the teachers two weeks before making the information public. The teachers were much happier — and so was I.

Program leaders, I've discovered, need a minimum of monthly communication, and perhaps as much as weekly visual contact with their teachers. As a pastor who is not directly involved with supervising the educational staff, my amount of needed communication is somewhat less. Most teachers do not expect the senior pastor to be intimately involved with their classroom, but any contact I make greatly builds my relationship with them.

No matter what size the congregation, pastors can do a number of things to build bridges to teachers. About three times a year, I ask one of the elders to take charge of the midweek service so I can sit in on the AWANA program. I'm not there to speak or critique. I may take part in a balloon relay with the kids, but my primary purpose is to chat with the leaders afterward, to sympathize with them about cramped facilities, and to affirm them in their important ministry.

I know other pastors who write a note of encouragement annually to each teacher, or who call each teacher once or twice each year, asking them for one classroom prayer request and one personal prayer request. All these involvements show that we're not only concerned with a good sermon. We also highly value the teaching ministry of each worker.

Esteem Teachers Publicly

When my wife was working on her master's degree, there was always a time when I could help with house cleaning, laundry, or dishes. I learned something about myself and the nature of people from those occasions. When she recognized and voiced appreciation of my work, I was open and even sometimes eager to do more work for her. However, when I put some of my own work aside to help her and my effort was not recognized, or I felt it was taken for granted, I found myself withdrawing and helping even less.

People continually wonder, *Does anybody care?* People need recognition. "I am willing to work with these junior highers, but does anybody notice?" Our availability and regular communication can go far to build that sense of appreciation. But in addition, we can take other steps to show we notice and care.

We sometimes highlight a department in the church newsletter or recognize the ministry of a specific teacher in the bulletin.

I mention in sermons interesting anecdotes from the classrooms that teachers tell me.

I also like to publicly pass along any compliments I hear. "I want to thank the Bible school workers, especially Pat, for their work this past week. I got three phone calls from parents who told me their children came home singing the songs they learned last week."

Or, in a sermon about how Bible study is not just intake but an opportunity for us to share the blessings we receive, I said, "I don't mean to embarrass Bev, but I learned this week she did exactly that. She was struck by two verses in the devotional she was reading, and when she went that day to visit Bill in the hospital, she wrote them on a small card. Bill told me later that they were just the verses he needed to hear."

How important is appreciation and recognition of staff. Its value is beyond measure.

In a hurting world, people need the healing words of the Great Physician. God has strategically assigned us to work in the church as resident chiefs of staff. Our involvement in the teaching ministry of the church extends beyond our own preaching. As we develop others who can teach and minister, we see what God intended the church to be.

JOB DESCRIPTION
SUNDAY SCHOOL TEACHER

DEFINITION:
Sunday school teachers shall be regular members of the church's educational faculty, with specific ministry in an assigned age-group class in the Sunday school.

RESPONSIBLE TO:
1. The Christian Education Committee.
2. The age-group Department Leader.
3. Appointed for a one-year term of service as noted on teacher contract.

SPECIFIC EXPECTATIONS:
1. Personal preparation of body, mind, and spirit.
2. Regular, systematic lesson preparation.
3. Knowledge of pupils, with interest in their everyday lives.
4. Consistent attendance at each unit teacher preparation meeting.
5. Regular, punctual attendance at the place of duty (arriving 15 minutes prior to starting time).
6. Weekly follow-up of absentees either through a phone call, personal visit, or a note.
7. Teaching as a regular team member of a department, using methodology that encourages student self-discovery.
8. Willingness to share in personal evaluations and department evaluations for the improvement of instruction.

QUALIFICATIONS:
1. A born-again Christian with a desire to grow in godliness.
2. A member of our church or in the process of considering membership.
3. One who nurtures his or her personal relationship with Jesus Christ through regular Bible study, prayer, and personal worship.
4. One who can commit the necessary time for personal preparation, staff meetings, and shepherding of the students.
5. One who supports the total church ministries of worship, teaching, missions, evangelism, and stewardship.

APPOINTMENT TO SERVICE
ON THE EDUCATIONAL FACULTY
"Trained Leadership for Transformed Lives"

Having received and approved your request for service at Trinity Baptist Church, the Christian Education Committee hereby extends to you an appointment to serve your Lord and Saviour, Jesus Christ, as

_____

until _____, 19____, at which time you may consider reappointment for another year.

As a worker in the educational program of the church, it is expected:
1. That you give of your best in the service you have accepted. Not exceptional ability nor outstanding qualifications, but faithfulness to the task assigned is of supreme importance.
2. That you attend regularly the planning meetings of your department or organization.
3. That you remember at all times that you are working with the lives of individuals, to help mold them after the life of the Son of God, as set forth in the Word of God.
4. That in public and in private you lead an exemplary life, honoring your Lord as well as having the best possible influence upon those you lead.
5. That you support the total ministry of the church, remembering the importance of each function.

"Therefore, my dear brothers, stand firm. Let nothing move you. Always give yourselves fully to the work of the Lord, because you know that your labor in the Lord is not in vain." 1 Corinthians 15:58

On behalf of the Christian Education Committee: Dated _____

_____, Chairman

_____, Ministry Director

_____, Teacher

FOURTEEN

TRAINING THAT MULTIPLIES

John Cionca

A

few years ago on a pleasant autumn evening, I was splitting the last of the wood that would carry me through the winter. As the sledgehammer crashed against the metal wedge for the umpteenth time, a piece of tempered steel flew off and lodged in my left thigh.

I went to our family doctor, a general practitioner. He made an incision and then used his probe to try and locate the metal. A little more cutting, and a little more probing. A little more cutting, and a little more probing. Nothing was said about an x ray. He finally closed the incision, unable to locate the metal chip. Today I still carry a scar of that trial-and-error experience.

In two weeks I am facing knee surgery I have put off for more than a decade. If I keep stalling, says a medical friend, I could be the proud recipient of a plastic knee down the road. So I've decided to take the step. A man in my congregation who had arthroscopic surgery recently has recommended his specialist, a highly trained surgeon with the University of Pennsylvania's sports medicine clinic.

Which doctor do you think I have chosen—my hometown G.P. or the specialist in Philadelphia? The answer is obvious.

Competence is valued in all professions. When your automobile has a carburetion problem, why do several friends suggest J & J Mechanics? The difference, even beyond natural ability, is training.

Pastors realize there is no short cut to competence. We want teachers to grow continually in the skills of teaching. We face several problems, however, in trying to provide training. For some churches, the cost of seminars, workshops, and materials is a hurdle. Others find the clock their worst enemy, not being able to find times when their people are available.

While these issues are real, I think the main barriers to training are something else. First, lay people do not perceive themselves as Christian educators but rather as regular folk who "just teach on Sundays." While at their employment they recognize the need for training, the same does not hold true at church. After all, they teach only an hour a week.

For some, it almost becomes a mystical thing. God surely will not allow Scripture to "return void." The Holy Spirit is supposed to do something with any text dropped on students.

In this kind of setting, the work of training teachers can feel like trying to push a rope.

A second problem is that local-church training programs are often sporadic. One pastor put it this way: "We need an ongoing training program, not just a one-time class for thirteen weeks."

In order to make our ministry team effective, we need to develop an overall training program, supported by continual encouragement of teachers to be part of that training. Here are some principles that, with time, can develop a program both accepted and utilized by a staff.

Build Right Attitudes

Pastors are models and motivators. We try to demonstrate Christian principles in our own daily living, and we try to encourage others to grow in Christ. If we want people to grow in their communicating skills, they must be aware that *we* are doing things to improve our pastoral skills. By sharing what we learned at a conference, passing on a good article, or summarizing a good cassette, we model the attitude that training is important.

Do we really believe there is no greater task in all the world than building God's Word into God's people? My family is important, sports have a place, and the grass must be cut, but there is no more worthy activity than taking the eternal Word of God and presenting it to the people of God.

Our program leaders have to catch our vision of that high calling. Whether someone teaches one hour or three hours a week is not the issue. What is significant is that in the time available they have the great responsibility and privilege of communicating reality and truth to people bombarded by society's illusions.

The teaching team may grow by hearing special conference speakers, but the ongoing excitement and motivation that moves them toward improving their skills has to be generated by us.

Use the Many Options Available

None of us in North America can say we lack training formats and materials. Here are the various components:

Curriculum. If a teacher wants to improve his or her skills, the place to start is to thoroughly study the teaching material. One church in our town has a particularly good early-childhood department. The coordinator believes it's because the teachers meet together, study the curriculum, and decide how they will apply it to their students.

Most publishing houses employ professional educators who understand learners and design methods to reach them. Volunteer teachers who ignore the curriculum only deprive themselves and their students.

Department Meetings. The boys of our church wanted a club program. Several men met for training, and there was an air of excitement. The club started out with much enthusiasm, but after four or five months something seemed to be missing.

As I checked with the program director, I recognized the problem. The men were no longer meeting for training and prayer now that the program was running. Each man was simply doing his thing. Loose ends were tied up through phone calls.

Regular program or department meetings are essential for planning and coordination, but they can also be used for building skills. When workers join together for prayer and program concerns each month, they enhance accountability and encourage fellowship among the ministry team.

If I could use only one training opportunity, the monthly department or program meeting would be it.

Individual Training. In the average college dorm, some students enjoy studying together for exams, while others prefer to isolate themselves in the library. In the same way, some teachers benefit greatly from a correspondence course, a book, or a tape related to their area of responsibility.

Our church has put together a list of good books and cassettes for teachers. Most are available in the church library, but I also keep copies of some. When a teacher is willing to work on his own, I provide the material, encourage him, and try to follow up later to let him know I'm proud of someone who invests personal time in the ministry of teaching.

Guest Speakers/Workshop Leaders. Last month I drove to Schenectady, New York, to spend Friday evening and all day Saturday with the teachers of a church. I really did not say anything I've not provided for my own people, but the very fact that I was an outside "expert" was motivational to that group.

When we provide opportunities for our teachers to hear excited educators, we not only give them bits of information to use in their teaching but also build their motivation for the Lord's work. I've personally known pastors who strengthened their educational programs by one or more of the following:

- Bringing in a consultant to do a Sunday school evaluation.
- Scheduling a Walk Through the Bible seminar, which was required for their teaching staff but also open to the entire congregation.

- Inviting a Christian education professor from a Bible college to conduct a Saturday morning seminar.
- Scheduling an evening for teachers to listen to a local expert speak on building self-esteem in children.
- Using a publishing-house consultant to help the staff implement their Sunday school material.

With some advance planning and scheduling, every congregation should be able to have at least one in-service training opportunity a year for its people.

Conventions and Seminars. When I was a freshman in college, our youth pastor took five of us a hundred miles to attend the InterVarsity conference on missions at Urbana. The sessions were meaningful to me, but equally special was the time I spent with Ed and these other committed collegians.

I've seen the same thing happen with Sunday school teachers as we've driven to weekend seminars 150 miles away.

The cost of these outside training opportunities varies from one to forty dollars per person. The value is well worth it. I don't have to be the expert; yet my people can be trained. I don't have to use my facilities, produce the materials, and manage all the other essential details; yet my people can have a full day or two of training.

When I take my people to such conventions, I notice other pastors are often absent. Yes, it is difficult for a senior pastor to get away—but no more difficult than for people who work at a secular job throughout the week. In the long run, I am much better off deferring six counseling sessions and attending a seminar with my teachers. My participation has a positive, multiplying effect. The time I spend in those training opportunities is far more beneficial than some of the repetitive, urgent calls that do not have a multiplying effect.

Develop a Comprehensive Program

What does all this add up to? Is there any way to coordinate the entire training effort? Can we be sure we are not omitting an important area? What can we expect and require of *every* worker?

I've been impressed with a homely little outline used by scores of churches called LEROY. In fact, I've used it successfully in two congregations. It was originally described in an article by Dr. Roy Zuck.

LEROY is an acronym for:

Leadership Training. To meet this requirement, workers complete a twelve-hour Christian education course—anything from a weekend seminar to a correspondence course to a night class at a nearby Christian college.

Evaluation. Here a teacher invites another person to evaluate one of his or her class sessions. Evaluations help us know how we are doing. Is this threatening? When everyone is doing it, the anxiety is minimized. Evaluators use a standard form. They are encouraged to be positive and supportive. At the end of the class session, they review their observations with the teacher and then leave the form with the person who has just taught.

Reading. To meet this qualification, the Christian education worker reads at least three hundred pages related to his or her area of teaching, chosen from an approved reading list drawn up by the Christian education committee.

Observation. This means going to watch *another* teacher at work. The program coordinator makes assignments and hands out observation forms to be used.

In one of my churches, I had a close relationship with pastors of two other congregations. We often had our teachers observe in the departments of one another's churches.

Yearly Conference. This criteria is met by attending a Sunday school convention and participating in one general session plus two workshops. (We permitted a substitution for those who couldn't make the convention weekend; they could study and outline three cassette messages from an approved list in the media library.)

The flexibility of this program is appealing. The requirements to be a certified worker are reachable by all. It doesn't matter if the person teaches on Sunday morning, leads a midweek club, or coaches a Bible quiz team. He or she can still be a LEROY worker.

For two months prior to introducing the program, we put signs around the church and in the newsletter that said, "LEROY is coming." Within four months of formal introduction, we had our first LEROY workers. Three individuals were presented with certificates in the morning worship service, and their pictures were placed in the narthex.

If such a program is to be effective, one person must oversee it. In our church, this person serves on the Christian education committee and maintains records of the entire faculty on four-by-six cards (see sample).

We've all heard the saying "If anything is worth doing, it is worth doing well. Pastors agree wholeheartedly. But there is no way to accomplish our task with our one to three shots of weekly preaching. In fact, our Lord knew this. That is why, through the influence of his Spirit, he told us our job was "the equipping of the saints for the work of service" (Eph. 4:12).

If our people are to be effective in teaching, we must give ample time and attention to team building. In fact, maybe this aspect of our ministry should be our highest commitment. I don't have all the skills to make my people effective biblical communicators, but those resources are available to me. They are all around me. My job is to plant seeds in the hearts of the Christian education committee and program leaders and keep cultivating them so they in turn can implement the details of ongoing training.

Teacher training doesn't need to be like pushing a rope. On the other hand, it will never be a self-propelled rope, either. We can *pull* a rope, however, thereby giving educational leadership to our churches.

I have not chosen my general practitioner to do the delicate arthoscopic surgery on my knee. Neither will parents choose to send their children to a Sunday school teacher who bores them and turns them off to the most exciting message in the universe.

While I can't do all things well, and some people might criticize me for deficiencies in my ministry, I choose to give attention and encouragement to ongoing teacher training.

SAMPLE LEROY BROCHURE

Questions and Answers

"What is LEROY?"
A five-part voluntary certification program for our Christian education workers.

"How can LEROY help me?"
*It is flexible and fully self-programmed. You can proceed at the pace best suited to you.
*It will broaden your training beyond "just another training course."
*It has built-in options to meet your individual needs and interests.
*It is easy for you to achieve and yet difficult enough to present a significant challenge.

"Why should I volunteer to earn the LEROY award?"
It will help you learn new methods to make the Bible relevant to today's students.
As you and others gain certification, the quality of instruction in the Christian education program will improve. Each person will be doing a better job for the Lord's glory.

"OK, how do I start?"
1. Look at the "Record of Progress" and decide which point of LEROY you want to complete first.
2. Write your name and date on the "Record of Progress" every time you complete a point.
3. Have your department head sign your "Record of Progress" when you complete all five points. Then give it to the minister of education. A properly signed and framed certificate will be presented to you in an evening service.
4. Each year thereafter, complete *one* of the five points to renew your certification.

RECORD OF PROGRESS

Leadership Course	name of course	your name	date
Evaluation	name of evaluator	your name	date
Reading	name of book(s)	your name	date
Observation	name of church	your name	date
Yearly conference	name of conference	your name	date

Office use:
Certification issued

_____
Signature of Department Head

EVALUATION OF THE
TEACHING-LEARNING PROCESS

This evaluation will necessarily be subjective; nevertheless, it
will serve as a useful tool in trying to analyze the teaching-
learning process. If you feel you are not qualified to make a
judgment on an item, you may omit it.

1. A general air of FRIENDLINESS pervades the classroom.
   Friendliness __:__:__:__:__ Coldness
2. The teacher's ENTHUSIASM stimulates class interest.
   Enthusiasm __:__:__:__:__ Boredom
3. The teacher uses PERSONAL EXAMPLES and is willing
   to admit personal shortcomings.
   Honesty __:__:__:__:__ Cover-up
4. HUMOR in the classroom tends to promote learning.
   Humor __:__:__:__:__ Lack of humor
5. Clear and commanding SPEAKING TECHNIQUE aids
   learning.
   Good speech __:__:__:__:__ Poor speech
6. Freedom from ANNOYANCES in the classroom contrib-
   utes to the effectiveness of the teaching-learning situation.
   Free from annoyances __:__:__:__:__ Many distractions

7. The PROMPTNESS and efficiency of the instructor increases the value of the class.

   Promptness __:__:__:__:__ Lateness

8. The general APPEARANCE and demeanor of the teacher are appropriate.

   Good appearance __:__:__:__:__ Poor appearance

9. The working relationship of the staff are complementary to each other and add to the UNITY of the learning process.

   Unity __:__:__:__:__ Disunity

10. The teacher maintains good DISCIPLINE in the classroom.

    Good discipline __:__:__:__:__ Poor discipline

11. The PURPOSE of the course is clear to the students.

    Clear purpose __:__:__:__:__ Unclear purpose

12. The instructor's PREPARATION appears adequate.

    Good preparation __:__:__:__:__ Poor preparation

13. Classroom activities are ORDERLY and systematic.

    Good organization __:__:__:__:__ Disorganization

14. ASSIGNMENTS are clear and challenging.

    Good assignments __:__:__:__:__ Poor assignments

15. Teaching METHODS are appropriate.

    Appropriate __:__:__:__:__ Not appropriate

    List methods used: *
                       *
                       *

16. Students PARTICIPATE actively in class procedures.

    Participate __:__:__:__:__ Do not participate

17. The class RELATES to daily life.

    Applicable __:__:__:__:__ Not applicable

18. The OBJECTIVES of the teacher were REACHED.

    Objectives reached __:__:__:__:__ Objectives not reached

19. Sufficient time is provided for REVIEW.

    Review time __:__:__:__:__ No review time

20. The teacher really LISTENS to the students.

    Listens __:__:__:__:__ Does not really listen

21. The authority in the classroom was:

    Word of God __:__:__:__:__ Teacher

Name of evaluator _____ Date _____

Form taken from *Make Your Sunday School Grow Through Evaluation* by Harold J. Westing (Victor, 1971). Used by permission.

FIFTEEN

THE FIVE THORNS OF CHRISTIAN EDUCATION

John Cionca

Have you ever been so far behind in your reading you've considered taking a speed reading course? The only problem was you could never find the time.

Most readers of this book are hustling from one ministry task to another. With few moments to spare, you are also trying to improve your ministry skills through study. That's why I want to get quickly to the things that trouble you most.

I took a long look at my own work in the church, then surveyed forty pastors at a denomination meeting for their common "thorns in the flesh" of Christian education. A few weeks later at an interdenominational meeting, I asked pastors to rank twenty Christian education difficulties. The top five were as follows:

1. Poor Follow-up and Visitation by Teachers

This afternoon I was visiting two elderly widows who are sisters and share a home. After an hour of cordial conversation and prayer, I was ready to leave. I suggested using the door on the porch, but one of the women led me to the door I had entered. She said jokingly, "Don't you know it's bad luck to come in one door and leave by another?"

While I'm not superstitious, I do know many churches suffer the consequences of people entering one door and leaving through another. One of the reasons is poor follow-up and visitation.

Here are four ongoing emphases that can improve the situation.

First, *try to staff the Sunday school with faithful, available, and teachable teachers*. Though some teachers (perhaps the old-timers) demonstrate that they are not open to change, we do have a choice when it comes to who we recruit. A worker who is faithful, available, and teachable will be open to someone explaining expectations, including proper follow-up of students.

The second thing is to *encourage the miniflock concept*. Teachers are not merely dispensers of Bible content; they are shepherds of a small portion of the congregation. I tell teachers they are more of a pastor to their students than I may ever be. I may carry the title, but in reality, the teacher who cares for them in an intimate way each Lord's Day and contacts them throughout the week has far more exposure. When a teacher realizes he is more than an instructor, follow-up will improve.

This responsibility cannot be expected of teachers if it is not spelled out clearly in the job description. As the teaching role is being explained, the potential education worker must become aware that care for the students is part of teaching.

A third ingredient for effective follow-up is *maintaining good records*. One church I visited had a detailed system that listed the name of every person who had ever attended or visited the Sunday school—even those who were now attending elsewhere, had moved, or even died. This was a waste of energy.

But I knew another church that kept no records at all. Several times the church office has wanted the name of a child but could not locate it. Even the teacher did not have the address or phone number. Visitors were not registered, nor did teach-

Dear Friends,

The Lord is doing much to build his church here at Southwood. Last Sunday while driving to our campus from the hospital, I noticed one of our members helping a woman whose car was stalled in the middle of Broad Street. I also rejoiced as another individual was willing to help Harriet Schifino with a need she had while convalescing with her broken elbow. The Rennies have mentioned how many people have expressed their love and concern for Amy. God has placed in our fellowship three hundred ministers, and it's encouraging to a pastor to see God's people using their gifts for his glory.

In the Love of the Savior,
Pastor John

A third thing we can do to minimize staff shortages is to encourage program leaders to *reduce the threat of teaching.* Roger was an automobile painter. If I were to ask him if he had the spiritual gift of teaching, or ask if he were a teacher, he would quickly say no. But Roger has worked in our kindergarten department for several years. He loves the children and they love him. We call him an "educational worker" rather than a teacher. (We use the terms interchangeably.)

Roger uses the Sunday school quarterly and works at one of the activity centers, but the scary word *teacher* is not ascribed to him. In this way he avoids a barrier that keeps others like him from service.

Fourth, it's important to *recruit properly.* Teachers who know what they are getting into are less likely to beg off at the earliest moment. Everything I've said about using job descriptions and teacher contracts applies here, for they increase the longevity of a teacher's service. That in turn reduces staff shortages.

Having *quality program leaders or department superintendents* is a fifth way to minimize shortage. A good program leader is an encouraging support to teachers before they get to the point of resignation. A superintendent named John was talking with Nick, asking how he and Debby were doing in the second-grade department. Nick said he was just about ready to quit because of three boys in the class. If John hadn't initiated the contact, Nick probably would have pulled his hair a few more Sundays and then resigned—lost from the educational faculty forever. By staying on top of the problem and encouraging Nick, a staff position was saved.

The last principle is obvious: *let teachers know they are appreciated*. One program leader listed in our newsletter the names of two couples who had just joined the teaching team. The point was to welcome them publicly to the children's division. In addition, the leader listed the other workers with the number of years they had been serving. The fact that Carol had been working nine years was significant, and printing it was both a gesture of appreciation and a note of information for the rest of the congregation.

Esteeming teachers should be natural. It's not like applauding a one-year-old who has stacked his blocks. As pastors and program leaders, we are filled with joy because people have caught the vision of building God's Word into God's people. Therefore, in all sincerity we take every opportunity to let them and others know how grateful we are for their service.

These principles are not a quick fix. They cannot guarantee sufficient staff for the next month. But systematic application of these attitudes and actions will alleviate the long-term, chronic condition of teacher vacancies.

3. Declining Sunday School Attendance

A number of years ago I served on the Christian education commission of our state association of churches. Each year the state director would pull out a Sunday school attendance graph that showed a continued decline from the previous year. He would charge us with coming up with a solution to reverse the defections.

The usual response was to set up a statewide contest or some other program to boost the statistics. That worked for some churches, but it really did not change the direction of the decline. I'm sure I sounded like a heretic when I suggested we tackle the problem through an ongoing teacher training program. You see, the fact was — contest or not — I did not want to send my children to most of those Sunday schools.

Not all churches are experiencing a decline in Sunday school. In fact, many have dynamic Sunday schools that are growing significantly. But interestingly, some churches that are growing in morning worship are simultaneously seeing a slight decline in their Sunday morning Bible school.

What are the causes?

Obviously, some congregations are experiencing a decrease in their overall church attendance. They have a smaller number of worshipers, and also an increasing absenteeism among attenders.

Other congregations have a maturing population. In earlier years their Sunday school had many children, but now—with society's fastest growing populations being young adults and senior citizens, they have a smaller potential clientele.

The diversification of church programming has also de-emphasized the Sunday school. Whereas once Sunday school was *the* educational program of most churches, now there are churchtime programs, choirs, clubs, and other specialties. The energy once given to Sunday school training and outreach has been diffused.

The purpose of some Sunday schools has also changed. The two main reasons for having a Sunday school used to be education and evangelism. Today, that has frequently evolved into education and fellowship. While fellowship is essential and is needed in our schools, the de-emphasis on outreach has created a corresponding decline in attendance.

Some Sunday schools show statistical losses because of a de-emphasis on busing, which was designed to reach neighborhood children. The long-term implications of reaching only children (not their parents) discouraged many from continuing this outreach. Whether busing had lasting spiritual effect is not the question here. What appears on the records are statistics, and the removal of this type of outreach program has affected the statistics significantly.

Some Sunday schools have been hurt by multiple worship

services. Whereas 9:45 A.M. was traditionally the Sunday school hour, worship services are now offered at 9:45 and 11:00, if not also at 8:30. Thus it is convenient for some parents to place their children in Sunday school while they attend the worship service—and then everyone goes home. Two of my own neighbors switched from the local Methodist church to the neighboring Presbyterian church because it offered this type of arrangement. They wanted to worship by themselves while someone else taught the kids.

For some families, the time of the Sunday school is now too early or too late. In our community, for example, I'm surprised at the extent of township athletics played on Sundays. With multiple worship services and Sunday school sessions, people can come to an early service and then leave early for the athletic event.

In light of these changes, I will dare to raise a new question: "What's wrong with a declining Sunday school?" After all, the Scriptures do not command us to have a growing Sunday school.

Now before you get me wrong, let me go on record stating I'm very pro-Sunday school. I make regular efforts to encourage members to participate. But the issue is not necessarily the Sunday school. Our commission is to teach all that Christ commanded. Whether the teaching takes place at 9:45 on Sunday morning or 7:00 in the evening is a secondary issue.

When I first began at this church, I was concerned to develop home Bible studies. At that time the midweek prayer meeting was the standard program. One home Bible study was begun, then another, then a third. Before long seven groups were meeting.

I was accused of selling prayer meeting down the river. The evidence seemed clear; whereas twenty to thirty used to attend, it was now down to twelve to eighteen. What my critics failed to realize was that the new format involved more than 120 people in weekly study.

The same principle applies to the Sunday school. While years ago a couple may have attended the Homebuilders class, now they attend morning worship service and a weekly home Bible study. In addition they may be listening to or watching Christian broadcasting.

I have no doubt that the pace and race of people, along with a growing apathy, has caused some to give up the two-hour commitment on Sunday morning. But when we look at the question of a declining Sunday school, we must place that alongside many other good programs that have been started for our people.

The best long-term answer (and maybe the only answer) for a declining Sunday school is a quality program that is relevant and vibrant. Most adults will not attend a boring and irrelevant Bible class; neither will they send their children.

Nevertheless, churches in declining neighborhoods, churches with an older clientele, or churches that offer multiple services and educational emphases may never have the Sunday school attendance of a past era. Every church, however, can have a vibrant education program.

4. Difficulty in Coordinating the Entire Program

Last Sunday an associate pastor from Australia visited our church. After the morning hour, we chatted about their ministry. He explained that, out of concern for overall coordination, he and the pastor write discussion questions about the Sunday morning message to be used throughout the week in their many home Bible studies. For that church, "coordination" means assuring parallel themes in several programs.

In another church, the couple who worked as junior high leaders were concerned that their midweek teaching "coordinate with Sunday school." What they meant was to make sure they were not covering the same thing. For them, "coordination" meant avoiding duplication.

Whatever a church wants to achieve in this regard, the place to begin is exactly the same. The most highly attended program is the hub. The teaching programs with the broadest exposure is where the balanced curriculum is planned. Other programs then plan their curriculum to supplement or vary from the primary program.

The greatest number of students in most churches hear the systematic pulpit teaching and the lessons in Sunday school. The majority of people participate in one or both of these.

As pastors we recognize the need for balance in our preaching, so we alternate between Old Testament and New, narrative and didactic passages, also covering poetry, parables, and prophecy. While some lean toward topical preaching and others toward systematic, verse-by-verse exposition, we still try to present the whole counsel of God.

Similarly, most publishing houses draw up a systematic plan for Bible coverage. They may move through the Bible in a conceptual way in the early childhood years. Then they recycle, with the focus on Bible stories or Bible history in the elementary years. The Bible is covered again in the youth years, followed by a mix of topics and book studies for adults. A church that does not use a Bible curriculum must develop a game plan on its own.

Although I don't know the exact direction of every sermon I will preach in the next four years, I have met several times with our adult Sunday school superintendent to coordinate my preaching schedule and the adult study subjects. Initially, we looked back fifteen years in the church's history to see what had been taught to our adults and what had not. Based on that list of previously given sermons and Sunday school electives, we set a tentative direction for both my preaching and the adult Sunday school.

Five years ago I knew I would be preaching from Ephesians, Joshua, Mark, Jude, Numbers, Romans, and Nehemiah. Likewise, the Sunday school knew the direction of the book studies and topical studies they would offer.

With this curriculum already determined, it has been easy to avoid duplication and yet to complement any given subject. For example, the coordinator of our women's ministries comes to me once a year to discuss possible subjects for ladies' Bible studies. By looking at the master plan, I help her see books or specific subjects to avoid because they are going to be taught soon in a larger program.

Prior to these systematic meetings, the women would just do their own thing. Three of the groups (approximately sixty women) had studied the Book of Joshua. One of our Sunday school classes was planning to study that book. In fact, the same student commentary was already ordered for the class. This type of overlap can now be avoided.

Another illustration of this principle can be seen in our club program. Once a year our Awana commander develops the main theme for the boys' council time. Again, knowing the flow of the third, fourth, and fifth grade Sunday school curriculum enables him to move to a different type of topical study that will interest the boys.

Not only can curriculum be coordinated, but so can the times of events and activities. While most churches keep a master calendar, regular communication of that master calendar to the program leaders is less often practiced. The master calendar should cause a two-way flow, thus letting the program leader know, for example, that four months down the road there will be a children's choir concert. This kind of early communication helps build a spirit of camaraderie among the workers in the fellowship.

5. Parental Apathy and Lack of Support

Is this a genuine defect among modern parents, or are there other explanations?

A primary concern to me is the pace of our families. It used to be just the medical doctor who was so busy we had to wait an hour to see him. Now even Grandma has so much on her to-do list that she is always behind.

In addition to Dad's hectic routine, Mom has now joined the work force or involved herself in several community activities. Some kids try to play soccer and football during the same season, while others take ballet, piano lessons, and are in the marching band at school. High demands are placed on our young people, especially by coaches, who view skipping a practice as a cardinal sin.

Sometimes in church we try to make our programs equally demanding. For example, one youth pastor set a standard that young people could miss only two practices if they wanted to be part of the puppet ministry. Two teenagers in that group were very busy with school activities but wanted to participate. The youth pastor stuck to his criteria and had a battle on his hands with two parents. From his perspective, the families were unspiritual; they let school activities have priority. From their perspective, the youth minister was unreasonable. One young man had participated in a sport for three years, and there was no reason he should drop out just to be part of the upcoming performance.

In another situation, a pastor visited a home where a family had started attending a different church. The two main reasons for leaving were: first, the time of the Sunday service was earlier, and second, their two high school boys didn't enjoy being put down every time they were absent. Both played football, and the high school teacher let them know how unspiritual they were to miss any of the youth programs because of their sports schedule.

We could probe for deeper reasons for what is called apathy: more mothers exhausted from work outside the home, the seductive influence of the media, and the prosperity of many families. A major cause of apathy is probably not home-based, however. The problem exists in the church itself. The services are repetitive, the sermons are boring, and the teaching is perceived as irrelevant. In many cases we might be our worst enemies.

What kinds of positive action can overcome the malaise?

The best way to get parental support is to *build a quality program parents believe is worth supporting*. Even though parents wish their kids would eat spinach, most will not continually force them. Neither are parents going to keep forcing their children to a program they abhor.

In contrast, a program that is upbeat, nonthreatening, enjoyable, and meaningful will more likely be desired by children and youth, and therefore, more readily receive parental support.

Second, *regularly teach the accountability of parents*. In preaching, through illustrations, even in Sunday school classes, we need to stress the church working hand in hand with the family. Eternal values must be presented on both fronts.

One wise youth worker frequently meets with parents and asks, "How can I help you with your responsibility to train your children?" He is siding *with* the parents against any family problems. He is not siding against the parents because of family problems.

Any congregation has some people who are on spiritual first base, some who have made it to second, and some maybe as far as third. None of us is home yet. Rather than crabbing at the person who is only on first base, we need to praise him that he joined the team, picked up a bat, and started on his way. We also encourage him to go to second. We encourage the person who has gone to third not to die there but to continue making progress toward home. In the long run, we accomplish more by painting a picture of the committed Christian than by complaining or heaping guilt on "apathetic parents."

SIXTEEN

DO YOU NEED A D.C.E.?

John Cionca

S ome churches wait until they can afford a staff expansion. Other churches stretch themselves, believing the expanded ministry will bring in the necessary giving units to support the salary.

Still others don't seem to need professional staff. Their lay people have administrative or educational backgrounds and effectively coordinate the C.E. program.

Some churches first expand to include a part-time staff member, while others go from nothing to a full-time person. Some hire a second generalist (an associate pastor), while others zero in on a specialist—a director of Christian education.

The expansion of staff in a church can be likened to the addition of a child to a family. For some the decision is easily made, while for others it takes a great amount of consideration. In any case, deciding is often less traumatic than when the newcomer actually arrives. That's when the tensions can sprout.

From Volunteers to Paid Staff

One church had trouble staffing its nursery for years. Many young families had been joining the fellowship, and now the church was moving into a third morning worship service. Many workers served every Sunday, while some worked only once a month or every three months. With three nurseries and six main services a week, the church was tying up scores of people each quarter in just one ministry. Young mothers, after being with their children all week, did not appreciate having to take a turn in the nursery. For them, singing in the choir or working in a girls' club was a welcome change.

The Christian education committee met to consider this growing need. While volunteer staff would always be part of their nursery ministry, the committee also felt it would be beneficial to hire a part-time attendant who would work every service.

The committee was also concerned for the children. Rather than being admitted to the nursery by different people at varying services, they would benefit from the friendly welcome of the same "grandmother figure" each time, which would help alleviate arrival anxieties.

The committee labored over its decision, for there was one woman they did not want to offend. She had worked in the nursery for ten years and felt it was her "baby." When the committee chairman asked for Lucille's input on the situation, she strongly opposed hiring someone. She offered to work a few more times a month to help prevent it.

When the decision was finally made, she drew her battle line. "The day an outsider is hired, I'll quit working in the baby nursery," she announced. She said she would be willing to move to the toddler nursery, but that turned out to be an empty promise. Lucille quit serving in that church eleven years ago, the very day the first nursery attendant was hired.

I often ask myself if it would have been possible to initiate the paid staff without losing that volunteer.

By contrast, I have seen a youth pastor added without sidelining the previous lay sponsors. I have observed the hiring of a music minister without losing the former lay choir leader. What enables a church to expand its staff smoothly? Here are some factors:

First, expansion must be a perceived need. The congregation must see that someone needs to develop and coordinate the overall educational program. It is not enough for the pastor or the board to see this. The congregation must own the idea as well. Part of my failure with Lucille was not helping her to see the seriousness of our staffing need.

Second, early and regular communication must precede and be maintained throughout the transition period. The congregation needs to be informed about the value of a minister of education. He or she is not going to replace the Sunday school superintendent, nor the librarian, nor the youth sponsor. The D.C.E. will be the equipper and resource for the educational team in order to have a growing ministry.

What a Minister of Education Can Do

A good Christian education minister will bring both qualitative and quantitative growth to the church. Quality will improve, because the curriculum, program, and staff all receive direct supervision. In a specialized way the D.C.E. is the encourager, team builder, and shepherd of the educational staff.

The minister of education will not only keep high quality in the existing program but also be sensitive to new program needs in the community or congregation. A competent person will, in a short time, produce a program that attracts additional singles and families. In a world that tries to lure people away from Christ, a strong Christian education ministry is greatly sought by parents.

As a pastor concerned with worship, preaching, missions, evangelism, stewardship, and education, I cannot keep abreast of the best materials or training possibilities for my people. As my church begins to grow and the programs expand, the help of a competent professional becomes strategic. Outreach and visitation have their place, but people will *continue* to come to a church only if something is worth attending. This obviously refers to the worship and preaching but equally to the Christian education program. When people are running out the back door as fast as they come in the front door, there is no growth. A competent minister of education helps prevent this.

The job description itself should be tailored to the church's specific needs, then adjusted according to the strength of the person hired. (Sample job descriptions appear at the end of this chapter.)

While some churches prefer job descriptions that include an accompanying "standard of performance," most are content to (1) define the job, (2) state primary relationships, (3) delineate specific responsibilities, and (4) express qualifications for the job.

In summary, the minister of Christian education is the executor of the church's educational program. While he or she reports to the senior pastor and serves on the Christian education committee, this person is the one responsible for ongoing implementation and coordination of the educational program. Styles of leadership among D.C.E.s are as varied as styles of leadership among senior pastors. Some are outgoing; others prefer to work behind the scenes. Nevertheless, effective ministers of education must have administrative skills as well as be able to work with people.

Hiring a D.C.E.

When Southwood Church considered expanding its pastoral staff in the area of Christian education and youth, we decided to seek a full-time person in this capacity. We were not close to any Bible colleges or seminaries; part-time possibilities were limited. We felt the Christian education ministry needed long-term oversight, and part-timers do not always stay very long. In addition, we had a need in both Christian education and youth, each of which easily could have been a full-time position.

Three options were available to the elders:

First, an individual from the congregation could be called for this service. Although there was one possibility, it did not appear to be the individual's leading or the search committee's preference.

The second option was to look for a professional currently serving on another church staff. This would allow the search committee to examine the person's track record.

In our case, however, we chose the third alternative: a new Bible college or seminary graduate. We were willing to be patient with a younger person and train him for the needs in our congregation. Finances were also an important variable; this was to be our third full-time staff member, and funds were limited.

A seasoned veteran would have consumed less of my time and would have been more effective earlier in his ministry. But a Bible college graduate, being younger and having fewer dependents, would be less expensive and would offer us an opportunity to train.

In marriage there seems to be a direct relationship between the length of courtship and success after the wedding. In the same way, the more knowledge the candidate and church have about one another prior to hiring, the more likely a successful tenure.

I have always had mixed feelings about asking a candidate to complete a Myers-Briggs test, a 16 PF, or the Taylor-Johnson Temperament Analysis. But at this point in my ministry, I believe it is important. Not only should the candidate be tested, but so should the pastoral staff, especially the senior pastor. A competent counselor can then be asked to look at the interrelationships of the staff to see how they mesh with the potential candidate. What interpersonal difficulties might be present? During the actual on-site interview, pointed discussion can be aimed at these potential problem areas.

I remember a seminar where results of a longitudinal study of a large school district were reported. Over a ten-year period, not one teacher had been terminated because of incompetence. The only firings had occurred over interpersonal relationships or personal behavior problems.

A clear job description, detailed items on reference forms,

on-site interviews prior to actual presentation of the candidate, and the use of psychological testing will help both sides discern the leading of the Spirit regarding a possible marriage in ministry.

Discipling the D.C.E.

As I have talked with ministers of Christian education, they have often seemed polarized when it comes to relationship with the senior pastor. Some feel they are little more than an errand boy for the senior minister's educational expectations and desires. Others feel the entire church program has been dumped on them: "You're the professional. . . . That's what we hired you for. . . . Whatever you think is best." This latter situation, in fact, seems to be more common than the first.

In my more hectic moments as a pastor, I'm prone to say, "I'm trying to play third base, shortstop, right field, and catcher all at once. At least the D.C.E. should be able to play first base without my help." But discipleship is an essential part of staff oversight. And it cannot take place without structure and regular contact. My relationship with the staff must be professional; therefore weekly or regular meetings for prayer and the sharing of ministry concerns is essential. My relationship with the staff must also be personal; therefore individual attention must be given, even if only over a cup of coffee during an informal moment of the day.

I have served on a pastoral staff where four of the ministers sang together in a quartet and played racquetball together three times a week. Because of common interests, our activities took us outside our professional relationship. I've also served on a staff where the three ministers were very different. One enjoyed classical music and tolerated some sports, one listened to contemporary music and hated sports, and the jock enjoyed the Sixteen Singing Men and the Blackwood Brothers. The professional relationship on that staff was cordial, but there was not a natural friendship that brought families together outside of our responsibilities.

Discipling the minister of education means helping the person be effective in his or her job. In one church our Christian education director was very teachable and creative, but he was not an initiator. That meant I needed to encourage Don and help him keep on top of the details of the education program. Often I would make suggestions, and Don was willing to implement them.

In another church our first Christian education director had great initiative, but he was not teachable. He viewed the slightest question as a slam on his competence and integrity. My ministry to Tom also had to be encouraging, but the relationship grew strained. It is hard to disciple an unwilling person.

In addition to weekly staff meetings, our staff gets away once or twice a year for a few days together. These days are spent studying a book, listening to tapes, discussing the ministry, and praying for the ministry and our families.

I also believe it is important for a pastor to encourage the minister of education to be involved with other Christian educators. If a D.C.E. participates in local college training clinics, visual-aid seminars, and curriculum presentations, he grows professionally and, in turn, so does the church's educational faculty.

Good discipling also includes regular evaluations. Every two years our associate staff receive an evaluation by the board of elders. This is based on the items in their job descriptions. The elders make honest commendations and recommendations for each responsibility. The periodic evaluations and especially the ongoing praise and feedback are important.

Adding a director of Christian education means I have one more person to whom I must minister. It also means, however, that there is another individual with whom I can share my heavy responsibility in the church.

Getting Caught in the Crossfire

It was only a few months after our new minister of education and youth had arrived that Terry and Joyce asked to see me. For two years they had been working as junior high youth sponsors. They were doing a fine job, but as laymen they were limited in the amount of time they could invest.

What troubled them now was Phil—his jocularity and sarcasm, for one thing. They also believed he was showing favoritism in the youth group, and that he always had to be the center of attention at every meeting. To a lesser degree I had made some similar observations. My first impression, however, was that Terry and Joyce may have been bothered because the new fellow on the block was winning the hearts of the young people.

Things came to a head a week later when Phil came to me and said he had just had a blowup with Terry and Joyce. He stated that Joyce was irresponsible; there was no way he could continue to work with her. She was continually challenging his authority and was only concerned with doing fun things with the kids. He felt he had no problems with Terry, but Terry would only continue to work if he and Joyce could work as a team. Phil had told them that wasn't an option.

Within twenty-four hours I was again meeting with Terry and Joyce, whose account of the blowup was completely different. They wanted to work with the young people, but Phil was being obnoxious and didn't want them. They felt they could not make the slightest suggestion to Phil without an explosive reaction.

After trying a second time with Terry and Joyce and with Phil and his wife, I finally saw that a change was necessary. In years past I would have wanted to choke both couples and tell them to get their spiritual act together. Brothers and sisters in the body of Christ ought to be able to live in harmony. While my theology hasn't changed, my understanding of depravity and personality differences has, and I view my role a little differently.

Now when I find myself in the crossfire, I try to follow these four principles:

First, *communicate early.* If I would have probed specifically in the area of Phil's staff relationships, some red flags would have come up earlier that may have helped me guide him with his ministry team. I could have helped him see that people's perception of a situation is as real to them as what is actually happening. Whether Phil was showing favoritism or not, the youth sponsors thought he was, and if he wanted to be an effective program leader, he had to deal with that. Early communication with him in these areas would have helped.

Second, when I'm caught in the crossfire, *my role is to be a peacemaker.* Whether or not I lose one party or the other, I must help both grow through the experience. I do not want to see Satan receive glory from disunity. I'd rather the Lord receive glory for averting a potential disaster.

My responsibility is to help my minister of education select the right staff and then minister to them. My task is also to help those who volunteer find meaning in their service. Honest confrontation, with a strong amount of encouragement, is needed for the peacemaking role.

A third part of my role is *getting people back on track.* That's why, as I talked with Terry and Joyce, I paid close attention to their sincere desire to serve the Lord. And they wanted to do it as a couple. For nearly a year we had been thinking about starting a college-and-career ministry. I painted a picture of that need and suggested they pray about it. Now, two years later, Terry and Joyce are still there, working with young adults, and glad for the opportunity to serve.

The last step, but sometimes the hardest, is for me to *get on with living myself.* I remember a locker room fight at a factory where I worked during my college days. The guy who got most beat up was the fellow who stepped between the two combatants. Sometimes I have been hit by the blows of criticism people aim at each other. Other times I find people on opposite sides of an issue thinking *I'm* the problem, and both begin to unload.

Some people blow up quickly but cool down equally fast. Others are not easily riled, but once upset, they have a harder time rebounding to normal. For the sake of my family, my health, and the other ministry responsibilities, I must put emotional issues behind me and go on living. After all, there will be another skirmish in the future. The soldiers might be different, but the scenario will be similar.

Terminating Ineffective Staff

I feel uncomfortable placing this subject in this chapter. I would like to think staff termination is a rare occurrence in the Christian church. Unfortunately, experience and discussions with pastors reveal that termination or unhappy resignations take place all too frequently.

Sadly, Terry and Joyce were not the only ones to experience tension with our minister of education and youth. Phil had troublesome encounters with the lay people who served as early-childhood coordinator, children's minister, Pioneer Girls director, and AWANA Club commander. Instead of being a resource person and giving leadership to these immediate subordinates, he was avoiding them. The problem was coming to a head.

Rigidity became a serious problem. A sixty-minute program could not be cut to fifty; a summer camping trip planned for twenty-two days "could not be shortened"; a retreat that ended at 7 P.M. could not end at 6 P.M. in time for the teens to share in the evening service. Even the suggestion that any of these changes be made was stubbornly challenged as a question of integrity, knowledge, or position.

Phil's unhappiness was growing, and he considered resigning. For five months he corresponded with other churches, but nothing seemed to open up. Knowing how important a first position is to an individual, I tried to be patient with him and help him grow in several areas. But his relationships continued to deteriorate, especially with the AWANA commander.

Two of our elders met with Phil and Hank to pray and help them work through their differences. As the elders later reported to the board, it wasn't the particulars that bothered them so much as Phil's inflexible attitude. He had already met with the elders for two evaluations. A program for his professional growth and development had been suggested. Unfortunately, little had changed. If anything, Phil seemed already to have resigned mentally from the position.

Although he wanted to stay on until he found a new position, the board felt this lame-duck situation was not healthy for the church. They suggested Phil resign in three months, with severance pay of up to two months beyond that.

In the interim, the board helped Phil with finances needed to take a course on interpersonal relationships. It was my hope that if change could be seen, termination might not be necessary. Such was not the case. Two years after Phil had come to our church, he left disillusioned and bitter.

I have been in the ministry for sixteen years and have served on four church staffs. Up to this time, I had never gone through this type of experience. As I talked with other ministers, however, I find the issue of terminating a staff member more common than I had realized.

As I have pondered this subject and interviewed both terminators and those who were dismissed, several suggestions have emerged:

First, *be continually honest and up-front with your staff.* Through the regular evaluations, weekly staff meetings, but more importantly, the personal times together, share your concerns for the person individually and for his or her ministry.

One C.E. director told me, "I wasn't aware there was dissatisfaction at all until the day Pastor Bill sat down and said, 'I have a biggie to share with you.' That was when he told me I needed to be looking for another position. It hit me like a ton of bricks.

"As a matter of fact, during the three and a half years of my ministry at that church, I had received nothing but positive feedback from Bill and those around me. That was not only in the form of personal compliments but also in significant pay raises."

Continual honesty with the staff and regular evaluations

help people know exactly how they are doing. They can re-chart their course—or start thinking about a change.

Second, *encourage people to support your staff.* On several occasions people invited Phil to dinner, and one home Bible study took a special interest in him. After his separation, some of these adults maintained contact with him. I encouraged two families to stay close to Phil, for I knew he would not believe my sincere desire for his well-being.

When I have asked terminated staff members what helped them get through their experience, almost always they have mentioned the support of significant people. In one case, a man from the former church stopped by every Wednesday on his way home from work simply to say hi and affirm the former minister.

Third, when possible, *encourage relocation after dismissal.* This is not always possible financially, but a geographical change is beneficial in the healing process for both the church and the staff person.

In one situation, an associate pastor moved out of state to do further graduate study. His new location and new energy-consuming involvement were psychologically helpful. In addition, a number of people in his new location were supportive. Within four months he was again ministering as pulpit supply in a small country church.

An opposite situation can be seen in two other ministers who have remained in their same depressive environments. One bought the home next to the parsonage, and almost daily either he or his wife bump into former parishioners. For a significant period of time he was out of work. He is now in secular employment, still working through his bitterness.

Fourth, *care for the physical needs of your former staff member.* It's tough to want to keep on supporting someone who is vocally critical and hostile to you personally and to the church. Nevertheless, in spite of getting your hand bitten even as you feed, you have a responsibility to care for the physical needs of the terminated minister. The family's needs are real. They did not sock away a large surplus while they were serving on the church staff, and relocation usually takes time.

The ongoing support is a tangible way to tell the embittered minister, "We really do care." To the congregation it says that while the person was ineffective on the staff, we are still personally supportive. I believe the Lord is honored by this.

I hope I haven't scared you off. A difficult staff relationship is always possible. But for most churches, the situation can be likened to a good Christian marriage. It takes work, but with it comes a deep joy and fulfillment. And it certainly beats being single.

I have been married in the ministry to three senior pastors, and more recently, I have been married to five associate staff members. The blessings and growth have far outweighed any disadvantages.

Many competent men and women are willing to serve the Lord and his church through Christian education. With thorough preparation of the congregation, careful recruitment, and regular discipling, the church can make great gains in its task of making disciples of all nations.

MINISTER OF EDUCATION AND YOUTH

DEFINITION:
The Minister of Education and Youth shall be a full-time member of the pastoral staff serving specifically in the church's educational and youth ministries.

RESPONSIBLE TO:
The Minister of Education and Youth shall be responsible to the Board of Elders, working directly under the supervision of the Senior Pastor.

SPECIFIC RESPONSIBILITIES:
1. Give administrative leadership to the total education program of the church.
2. Serve as an ex-officio member of the Christian Education Committee, working with the committee to develop educational aims, policies, and program.
3. Assume supervisory responsibility for the education program and devote sufficient time for the development of Bible school, Sunday school, children's churches, club programs, and youth activities. This means counseling with superintendents, youth leaders, teachers, officers, and organizations, evaluating their work and offering suggestions for improvement.
4. Serve as youth coordinator for advisers working with junior high, senior high, and college-career adults.
5. Assume responsibility for midweek Bible studies, active social and recreational programs, visitation programs, and special outreach programs for young people.
6. Build relationships with young people, and be available to counsel teens and parents.
7. Promote and publicize developments in the education and youth program.
8. Work as a team member of the pastoral staff in areas of general pastoral duties.

QUALIFICATIONS:
1. A born-again believer, in accord with the church's constitution.
2. Spiritually mature, maintaining personal Bible study and prayer.

3. A pastoral heart with a burden for local-church ministries.

4. Gifts and abilities in the area of Christian education and youth.

5. Ability to work with people.

6. Supports the total church program of stewardship, worship, missions, fellowship, and education.

MINISTER OF CHRISTIAN EDUCATION

DEFINITION:

The Minister of Christian Education is a member of the professional staff who serves as a director of the educational program of the church.

RESPONSIBLE TO:

As a member of the professional staff, the Minister of Education is responsible to the church through the Board of Deacons. His personal ministry shall be under the supervision of the Senior Pastor. He shall also be an ex-officio member of all committees relating to his ministry area.

SPECIFIC RESPONSIBILITIES:

1. Work with the Associate Pastor as a supervisor, administrator, promoter, and developer of the Christian education program of the church.

2. Be directly responsible for children's ministries (preschool through sixth grade) and adult ministries.

3. Meet regularly with the pastoral staff to coordinate the program of Christian education with the total ministry of the church.

4. Seek, in cooperation with the pastoral staff, to create a concern for Christian education throughout the church, promoting the aims and goals of each agency through preaching, teaching, and the printed page.

5. Seek to discover, enlist, and train workers for the many agencies under his supervision.

a. Encourage workers to further their growth in spiritual and technical knowledge through attendance at workers' conferences, training courses, private reading, personal Bible study, daily prayer, and if possible, Bible classes.

b. Provide a regular program of leadership training to instruct workers in each agency.

c. Provide help and counsel to workers on the job.

6. Give guidance and counsel to the Christian Education Committee members, assisting them to fulfill their responsibilities.

7. Be responsible for reviewing and evaluating all curricula.

8. Examine both building and equipment regularly to see that all is in order.

a. Take the initiative in recommending and securing additional equipment that would lend itself to more efficiency.

b. Consult with the pastors and appropriate boards when additional equipment or space is deemed necessary for growth.

9. Work with the visitation minister to promote a program of visitation, growth, and outreach. Children's visitation shall take place though the existing structure of Sunday school and weekday clubs.

10. Work with the Associate Pastor to promote a family ministry that emphasizes the importance of the home in Christian education and spiritual growth.

11. Serve as a resource person to all personnel of the educational faculty and therefore shall keep informed of educational techniques, materials, and programs through private study, personal associations, and professional conferences.

QUALIFICATIONS:

The Minister of Christian Education must fulfill the spiritual qualifications of elder set forth in the Word of God, for he is a minister of the gospel serving in a specialized area. He must be called of God, a student of the Bible with adequate professional training in religious education. He must be thoroughly in accord with the church covenant and constitution, and must support the total church program of worship, teaching, missions, fellowship, evangelism, and stewardship.